SCANDINAVIA

WESTERN EUROPE: ECONOMIC AND SOCIAL STUDIES

Series edited by Eleonore Kofman and Allan Williams

Western Europe: Economic and Social Studies is a series of introductory texts dealing with the major countries of Western Europe. It provides a concise overview of the economic and social geography of individual countries or areas, using contemporary social science theories to interpret the evolution of geographical patterns. Each book covers the political and economic context; post-war economic and social development; rural transformation; urbanization; regionalization; future development, and includes a detailed bibliography. Each is suitable for use on a range of courses, including geography, language, economics and social science.

The United Kingdom   Ray Hudson and Allan Williams
France   Eleonore Kofman and Chris Flockton
Italy   Russell King
Ireland   Barry Brunt

Brian Fullerton was Senior Lecturer in Geography at the University of Newcastle upon Tyne until 1989, and had previously taught at the Universities of Glasgow, Alberta (Canada) and Århus (Denmark). His main interests are in economic and regional geography, particularly transport and Scandinavia.

Richard Knowles is Lecturer in Geography at the University of Salford and has also taught at the Universities of Birmingham and Simon Fraser (Canada). His main research interests are in transport and political geography, and in Scandinavia.

SCANDINAVIA

BRIAN FULLERTON
Former Senior Lecturer in Geography,
University of Newcastle upon Tyne

RICHARD KNOWLES
Lecturer in Geography,
University of Salford

WESTERN EUROPE:
ECONOMIC AND SOCIAL STUDIES

P·C·P
Paul Chapman
Publishing Ltd

ACKNOWLEDGEMENTS

The authors would like to thank Lois Judge, Olive Teasdale and Christine Warr for drawing the figures, Moira Armitt and Marie Partington for word-processing, the Press and Information Offices of the Danish, Norwegian and Swedish Embassies in London and also Eleonore Kofman and Allan Williams for their sound editorial advice on the final text. The ultimate responsibility for any errors or omissions, however, rests with the authors.

Paul Chapman Publishing Ltd
144 Liverpool Road
London
N1 1LA

British Library Cataloguing in Publication Data
Fullerton, Brian, 1928–
   Scandinavia. – (Western Europe: economic & social studies)
   I. Title II. Knowles, R. (Richard D.), 1947–
   III. Series
   330.948

ISBN 1–85396–083–7

Typeset by Setrite, Hong Kong
Printed in Great Britain by Athenaeum Press Ltd, Newcastle upon Tyne.

CONTENTS

ONE

The Scandinavian Framework

1.1 Introduction

Scandinavia has long been the accepted name for the large European peninsula between the Baltic and the North Atlantic. During the nineteenth century, as political boundaries took precedence over physical features, Denmark was included in Scandinavia. Although living on a peninsula of the North European Plain, Danes have had much more in common with Norwegians and Swedes than with Germans. Finland has had close historical, political and social links with Sweden (despite a fundamentally different language) but is not discussed here since its complex relationships with the USSR are beyond the scope of a book of this length.

In fact, Denmark, Norway and Sweden lie at the centre of a wider grouping of states and island territories that collectively refer to themselves as *Norden* — the North. All these countries were originally settled and/or politically organized by Scandinavian-speaking peoples. From the eighth to the tenth centuries the Scandinavians planted colonies on the Atlantic Islands and Greenland, in the British Isles and northern France. They founded the city states of Novgorod and Kiev in the Russian lands and incorporated interior Finland into Sweden. While the Scandinavian colonists in Britain and Russia were eventually absorbed by the native peoples, the rest of the Scandinavian world was united under the Danish crown in 1389.

A separate kingdom was set up in Sweden in 1523. During the seventeenth century Sweden annexed parts of Denmark and controlled most of the southern and eastern Baltic coastline. The nineteenth century saw a further political disintegration of the Scandinavian kingdoms. In 1809 Finland became a Grand Duchy within the Russian empire. A strong Swedish legal and cultural inheritance was retained but the Swedish language was gradually replaced by Finnish in education and administration. Finland became an independent state in 1918 (with the Åland Islands as a self-governing, Swedish-speaking province). Norway was separated from Denmark in 1814 and gained home rule, but was forced into a united kingdom with Sweden that lasted until 1905. Iceland became self-governing in 1918 and severed all political links with Denmark in 1944. Greenland and the Faroe Islands are now self-governing and outside the European Community (EC) but continue to send representatives to the Danish parliament. The increasing co-operation of the independent states of the North in economic and social affairs since the Second World War is discussed in section 1.4 below.

Denmark, Norway and Sweden (Figure 1.1) are three of the richest and most egalitarian countries in Europe. They are characterized by fully comprehensive education and health services, high taxes and narrow wage differentials. Norway and Sweden have enjoyed virtually full employment throughout the economic vicissitudes of the last twenty years. One hundred and fifty years ago, however, Denmark, Norway and Sweden were among the poorer European states, peripheral to the continent, suffering unfavourable winter climates and lacking a sufficient range of natural resources.

The rise of the Scandinavian countries from relative poverty to relative wealth, compensating their geographical disadvantages by pragmatic and rational policies and the steady expansion of education and public participation in decision-making is summarized in section 1.2 (for a fuller discussion, see Hodne, 1975; Jörberg, 1973; Jörberg and Krantz, 1975; Mead, 1981). This book outlines the development of the characteristic political institutions and social structures of the Scandinavian countries over the last thirty years: how they were affected by the 'cold war', the economic expansion of the 'happy Sixties' and economic setbacks during the 1970s.

The growing internationalization of trade and investment and the development of the EC towards a single market and perhaps even a common currency pose severe problems for the Scandinavian peoples. Their originally independent economies, each concentrating on the export of a limited range of raw materials and food products, are now more complex and are dominated by their service and manufacturing sectors. But even the combined Scandinavian market of 17 million people is not large enough to support the sophisticated domestic industry and agriculture that maintains high living standards. Some imports are essential and export markets must be found to pay for them, most notably within the EC. Competition in foreign markets requires a constant adjustment of production to world market forces. The extent to which the Scandinavian states succeed in developing international trade and specialization within as large a market as possible and, at the same time, maintaining political independence, the characteristic structures of Scandinavian society and an equitable spread of the benefits of economic development across all classes and regions will have important lessons for other developed economies.

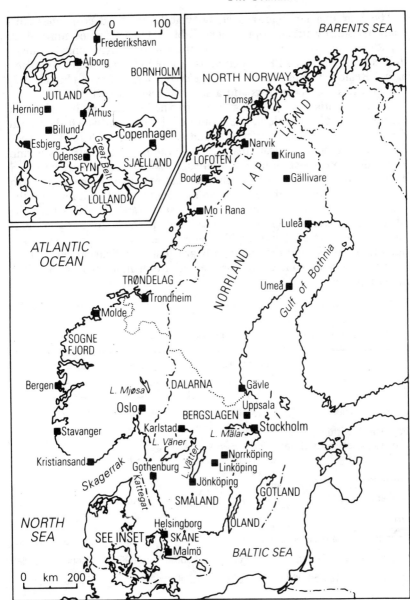

Figure 1.1 Towns and regions

The Scandinavian countries enjoy typical developed economies with characteristically urban populations (Table 1.1). About one third of all Scandinavians live within 50 km of one of the four conurbations. Denmark differs from Norway and Sweden in its lack of extensive thinly populated areas. Relatively long distances between the larger towns (Figure 1.2) lead to extra transport costs and a sense of regional particularism.

Social scientists used to argue as to whether the traditional social organizations of a people or the nature of the land on which they lived did most to determine their culture and economic life. There is evidence for both arguments in Scandinavia, where the natural constraints within which decisions must be taken are greater than in most other developed countries. Twentieth-century civilization has not changed the long, harsh winters, nor colonized the Norwegian mountains, nor found much in the way of new opportunities for the vast forested plateaux of Sweden. The islands of the Danish archipelago are still only partially linked by bridges. North Sea oil and gas have provided a new energy balance in recent years but will not satisfy entirely the rapidly growing Scandinavian demand for energy nor wholly compensate for the planned abandonment of Swedish nuclear power.

Table 1.1   Scandinavia − area and population, 1988

	Denmark	Norway	Sweden	Scandinavia	
Area (km²)	43,093	323,878	449,964	816,935	
Population (000s)	5,100	4,200	8,500	17,800	
Population within 50 km of Copenhagen/Malmö/ Helsingborg	1,700		800		
Stockholm			1,500		
Gothenburg			700		
Oslo		1,100			
Four major conurbations				5,800	(33%)
Other towns, > 50,000	600	500	2,500	3,600	(20%)
Other towns, 10−50,000	800	1,200	1,400	3,400	(19%)
Remainder	2,000	1,400	1,600	5,000	(28%)

Sources: *Yearbook of Nordic Statistics* (1981, 1988 and 1989−90); national censuses.

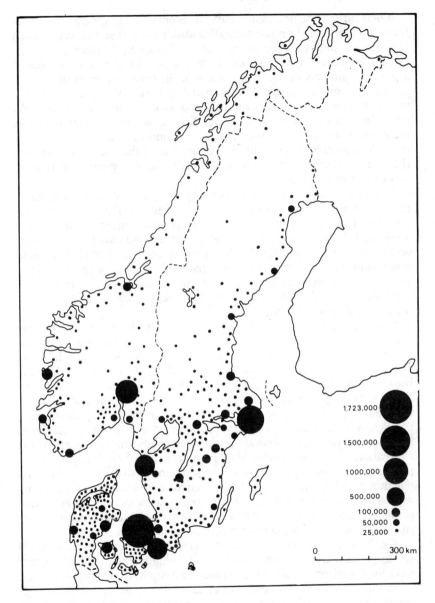

Figure 1.2 Population distribution

When agriculture dominated national economies, geographers concentrated their attention on the natural conditions of soil and climate, which favoured or inhibited the development of particular farming systems. Urbanization, the growth of manufacturing and the later development of a predominant service sector has led to an increasing interest in the way in which decisions affecting the spatial patterns of the economy are taken, and also in political structures and social institutions. This book, like others in the series, focuses attention on where and how decisions are made and who makes them. It is also concerned with the impact of these developments on the internal geography of the northern countries, the distribution patterns of their population and regional contrasts in wealth and opportunity.

The long-standing pursuit of equality of opportunity and consensus has by no means obliterated regional differences. The range of Scandinavian life-styles still includes cosmopolitan entrepreneurs in the wealthier suburbs of Copenhagen and Stockholm and God-fearing crofters on remote Norwegian islands. Scandinavia and the British Isles have some similarities as semi-detached parts of Europe with their best-endowed territories nearest to the continental mainland. There is also a somewhat parallel history of alternating *rapprochement* and aloofness towards mainland Europe.

Visitors to the Scandinavian countries from North America or Western Europe find a great deal that is familiar, but the longer they stay and become aware of the social and economic life around them, the more they will recognize a set of distinctive Scandinavian attitudes (which are broadly shared with the other northern nations, Iceland and Finland). Scandinavians give a rather higher profile to equity and justice in the allocation of resources and employment than most English-speaking peoples. The Scandinavian concept of democracy differs from that held in much of the English-speaking world by preferring consensus to the alternation of governments based on political parties with widely divergent programmes. A strict proportional representation of votes to seats therefore operates at all levels of elected government and a variety of views are represented on the boards of administrative agencies. Co-determination is well established in manufacturing industry: workers' representatives sit on the boards of management of many companies.

The Scandinavian countries are widely recognized for their political stability, economic affluence and social enlightenment. Their history since the Napoleonic Wars could be read as a continuous story of progress in these three characteristics and a justification for those outstanding nineteenth-century Scandinavians such as Grundtvig, Dalgas, Ericsson and Nansen, who, in their different ways, had visions of what was possible and worked so hard to realize them. In fact, success has always depended upon three equally important conditions: European peace; access to foreign markets (in order to enable the Scandinavians to specialize on their narrow industrial base and the skills of their highly educated but expensive workforce); and a broad domestic consensus on political, economic and social structures. Scandinavian governments have always done what they could to defend their integrity and to foster free trade and peace in Europe, although their detailed policies have varied with their individual conceptions of contemporary circumstances. As small countries in a shrinking world and on the borders of more powerful political entities such as the EC and the Soviet Union, their progress has been partially determined by the policies of foreign governments.

The industrial economies of Scandinavia are robustly capitalist. The role of the State in regulating and subsidizing private industry has always been limited and has declined significantly during the 1980s. Taxes on industry are modest and there are important tax reliefs for investment and saving. The public sector is larger than in most English-speaking countries, absorbing up to two thirds of the gross domestic product (GDP). High levels of private taxation fund health, education and other social services and provide subsidies for many public transport services. Taxation policies intended to reduce disparities of income have, however, had little impact on differences in wealth.

The Scandinavian concept of the Welfare State is one in which all citizens have the right to high standards of education and health care and to a decent standard of living, which, if not available out of personal income, may be supplied by State agencies. Welfare is a right, available to the whole population, and is not restricted to targeted groups such as the poor, pensioners or recent immigrants. The receipt of welfare does not depend on previous individual contributions or on insurance principles: welfare is largely funded from tax revenues. The education and health services (discussed in Chapter 5) are universally available and used by almost everyone. Most Scandinavians argue that welfare services would deteriorate if they were not universal because the wealthiest and most influential citizens would no longer be personally involved in them.

The main constraints on Scandinavian policy-making arise from their internal constitutional arrangements and the need to take account of developments abroad, especially within the EC, the Soviet Union and the international trading community. It is important for readers in English-speaking countries to appreciate significant differences among North American, British and Scandinavian democratic constitutional practice. The characteristic social and political structures of Scandinavia are therefore discussed in section 1.2 below. Section 1.3 outlines the economic vicissitudes of the Scandinavian states over the last thirty years, and section 1.4 discusses the economic integration of the northern countries,

Scandinavian international trade and initiatives in the Third World. Section 1.5 describes the physical geography of Scandinavia. Internal economic and social issues are explored in more detail in Chapters 2–5, while Chapter 6 reviews current problems and prospects.

No book of this length can do justice to the detailed complexities of Scandinavian economies and societies. Books in English upon particular aspects and individual countries appear rather rarely, but readers in search of greater detail, a longer time perspective or a different conceptual approach are recommended to Mead (1958), Sømme (1960), John (1984) and Varjo and Tietze (1987) for geographical surveys of the whole region, and to Connery (1966), Derry (1979) and Mead (1981) for further political and historical background. Glyn Jones (1986) and Rydén and Bergstrom (1982 – Sweden), Hodne (1983 – Norway) and Johansen (1986 – Denmark) provide useful historic and economic surveys of individual countries. Urban perspectives may be found in Falk (1976 – Sweden) and Torstenson, Metcalf and Rasmussen (1985 – Norway).

1.2   Traditions of government

1.2.1   *Structures of government*

After periods of autocratic government in the seventeenth and eighteenth centuries, the Scandinavian states became constitutional monarchies during the nineteenth century. A steady process of constitutional revision gradually transformed them into parliamentary democracies with universal suffrage and proportional representation.

Because of the similarities of their language and culture, each Scandinavian country has been strongly influenced by the development of political institutions and movements in the others. All have written constitutions that define the structure of government in considerable detail. In many respects governmental structures are closer to those of continental Europe than those of Britain or North America. Their parliaments have one chamber (in Norway the elected members divide into two groups to discuss legislation). Elections take place at least every four years in Denmark and Norway and every three years in Sweden. The Norwegian parliament cannot be dissolved between elections. In Denmark and Norway the crown, and in Sweden the speaker of parliament, presides over the formation of governments.

The level of political interest is very high, with over 80 per cent of the voters normally voting in general elections. Power is more evenly balanced between political parties and interest groups than is usual in most English-speaking democracies. Party loyalties are very strong among the voters and parliamentary landslides are virtually unknown.

Scandinavian parliaments are ultimately sovereign in so far as they can amend the constitution if this is repeatedly demanded by a majority of voters, but they exercise less detailed influence on short-term policy than English-speaking parliaments. The political composition of parliament determines who shall make policy since the ministers, who form the cabinet, are drawn from the majority party or from a coalition that can command a majority. State constitutions identify about a dozen policy areas and specify one or more ministries and parliamentary committees for each one. Ministries are relatively small policy-making bodies since administrative agencies administer the laws and apply their principles to individual cases. The boards of management of the administrative agencies include representatives of the political parties, trades unions, employers' organizations and other interest groups. Agencies are responsible to the cabinet as a whole and not to their own minister. State utilities (such as Swedish Rail) may operate as commercial enterprises, deriving a proportion of their revenue from the State. There are also State-owned enterprises (e.g. Statoil in Norway).

Most of the work of parliament, especially the drafting of new laws, is done in parliamentary committees on which the political parties are represented in proportion to the number of seats they hold. It is normal to hold wide consultation with all interest groups before new policies are introduced, and Royal Commissions of Inquiry play an important part in influencing public debate. Consultative national referendums may also be held on such issues as the eventual abandonment of nuclear power, as in Sweden in 1980. In Denmark, a referendum must be held on proposals for constitutional change (such as joining the EEC in 1972 and signing the Single European Act in 1986). The press has strong constitutional guarantees, which enable it to act as a watchdog over government. The office of *ombudsman*, an independent investigator of complaints against maladministration, was first established (in Sweden) as early as 1713.

Scandinavian local government is a complex hybrid of national and local interests. Figure 1.3 shows the location of the counties (*amt, fylke, län*), which are subdivided into municipalities (*kommuner*), and which are comparable in some respects to English districts. Responsibilities vary in detail between the three countries but the Swedish structure, described below, typifies general Scandinavian practice. County and municipal councils, similar to those of Britain, each have defined responsibilities for the provision of utilities, health care, education, public transport and social assistance. In contrast to Britain, municipal councils are not subordinate to county councils. The welfare services are financed through local income taxes and some charges for services. Local authorities may also receive equalization grants from national government to help them carry out their obligations to provide essentially similar levels of welfare in all parts of the country.

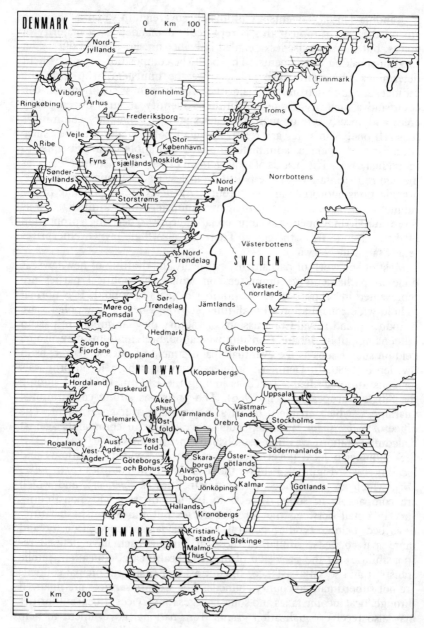

Figure 1.3 Counties

The national government also operates at county level through a governor and County Administrative Board, whose members are jointly appointed by national and local government. This board collects taxes, maintains public order, co-ordinates physical planning and regional development policies, hears appeals against decisions by statutory committees and represents the interests of the county to the national government. There is a parallel link between national and local governments within the political parties and it is not unusual for members of parliament also to sit on county and municipal councils. The identification of Scandinavian members of parliament with the local interests of their constituencies is not as strong as in Britain or North America since constituencies are based on relatively large regions rather than on local areas.

The national administrative agencies operate at county level through County Executive Boards appointed by national and local government and by the agencies concerned. Some executive officials are responsible both to the county council and to a national administrative agency. Political parties are normally represented on local government executive committees in proportion to their votes. As a result of proportional representation, single-party control of county and municipal councils is not as usual in Scandinavia as in Britain, but the practice is spreading in Sweden (Gustafsson, 1988).

As in Britain, population changes, the growth of car ownership and the development of services have led to a complete re-organization of local government in each of the Scandinavian countries since the Second World War. Danish county boundaries were redrawn in 1965 and in all three countries county councils were given greater powers and responsibilities. Within each municipality a central town was chosen as an administrative service centre where the general hospital, high school and main transport centre are normally found. In rural Norway, with its thinly dispersed population, some municipalities cover very large areas with more than one potential service centre, and there have been some bitter rivalries between towns for specific municipal services. Large cities have special administrative status and, where they have spread over county boundaries, there are passenger transport authorities.

1.2.2 *The social framework*

The success of the Scandinavian countries in becoming wealthy while maintaining a high degree of liberty, equality and fraternity owes much to a series of historical developments that have also resulted in a considerable homogeneity among Scandinavian populations. The ancestors of the Scandinavian people were already settled there when written history began and no subsequent invasions (such as the Norman conquest of the

British Isles) have established the hegemony of a new ruling group. The feudal system did not develop as strongly in Scandinavia as in Western Europe and the class of land-owning, tax-paying peasant farmers was larger and more influential in local affairs. In 1500, for example, half the cultivated land of Sweden was owned by peasant farmers. The union of the crowns in 1389 left Norway without the focus of an hereditary monarchy and court for nearly six hundred years, and Sweden for two hundred.

The slaughter of the Swedish nobility by the Danish king in 1520 left a power vacuum, which enabled the surviving Vasa family to re-establish the Swedish crown and develop a strong bureaucratic State. At about the same time the Reformation delivered the wealth of the church to the Danish and Swedish crowns. Scandinavia experienced autocratic government in the seventeenth and eighteenth centuries: religious and political dissenters were exiled. The feudal powers of the nobles and the other estates were largely replaced by highly centralized national governments in which many noble families became almost hereditary civil servants. The privations of war and, in Denmark, of invasion, subjected the great majority of the population to a low subsistence economy, reinforcing the ancient customs by which food, shelter and inherited property were shared among members of a family.

When political and economic liberalism finally arrived in the mid-nineteenth century, most people were still living on the land. Equal inheritance rights hampered the development of either a landed aristocracy or a commercial plutocracy. A small number of families were able to acquire wealth in mining, forestry, manufacture and overseas trade. Their power was constrained by reliance upon foreign markets and on their need for foreign capital, which was channelled through State loans. Agricultural overpopulation in the forest areas of Norway and Sweden was relieved by substantial emigration to North America during the latter half of the nineteenth century. Elsewhere a slow movement to the towns, and the internal colonization of previously poor agricultural land in Jutland and northern Sweden, relieved rural population pressures and maintained farms of viable size. In marked contrast to Western Europe and North America there were no immigrations of unskilled workers with different traditions.

The Lutheran churches, which were instruments of the State, reaching into every parish with a message of conformity and obedience, also actively fostered education and literacy among the whole population. Well-educated Scandinavians became proficient in the main languages of Western Europe and travelled widely. The works of Ibsen, Kierkegaard, Strindberg, Münch, and others reflected the tension between the revelations of a wider world and the stifling conformity of daily life in much of Scandinavia. The Scandinavian intelligentsia were fully aware of West European ideals of democracy, co-operation and socialism and of their potential for Northern Europe.

During the second half of the nineteenth century – a period of industrialization and acute rural distress – a number of popular movements emerged, including trades unions, producer and consumer co-operatives, a temperance (alcohol prohibition) movement and a spate of evangelical revivals that led to the establishment of largely self-governing 'missions' within the national churches. Strengthened by the Folk High School movement for adult education in Denmark and its imitators in Norway and Sweden, these popular movements encouraged education and self-education. They also gave industrial workers, small farmers and their families experience in organizing themselves into legal opposition to the established hierarchies of civil servants, large land-owners, industrialists and clergy.

In rural Norway a popular movement arose in the 1850s to establish a distinctive Norwegian language based upon the dialects of western and upland Norway. At that time Norwegians spoke a variety of dialects but wrote in a modified Danish. The new language – *Nynorsk* or *Landsmål* – is officially used today in many parts of Norway, while *Bokmål* or *Riksmål*, which, in its written form, retains greater affinities with Danish, is widely used in the large towns and in south-eastern and northern Norway. The language movement gave powerful grassroots support to the nationalist cause, which eventually succeeded in dissolving the union with Sweden peacefully in 1905. Almost all these popular movements supported the extension of the vote to the whole adult population, which was finally achieved in 1920.

Popular movements still play an important role in Scandinavian political life. The most important are the trades unions (Sweden being the world's most highly unionized industrial State with 82 per cent of the labour force enrolled in either a blue collar (LO) or white collar (TCO) affiliated union). After the First World War conflict between employers and trades unions escalated until a dangerous confrontation in Norway and the shooting of some Swedish workers during a strike in 1931 shocked the protagonists to the conference table. The Swedish Saltsjöbaden Agreements of 1936 provided a model for annual meetings between employers and unions to decide norms for national wage increases. In this way the Scandinavian countries pioneered one of the major elements of social consensus that developed in the Western world after the Second World War. The white-collar unions grew rapidly during the 1960s with the expansion of service industries. In 1988, 82 per cent of the labour force in Sweden, 72 per cent in Denmark and 60 per cent in Norway were union members (compared with 40 per cent in Britain and 17 per cent in the USA). Since 1973 in Norway (1976 in Sweden) workers have been represented on the boards of directors of companies with more than 25 employees. The trades unions are also widely represented on the boards of administrative agencies.

Popular movements are regularly consulted when legislation is being prepared, and they are represented on the boards of administrative agencies. This official recognition has facilitated the rapid advancement of women into Scandinavian political life in parallel with their increased participation in the workforce since the 1950s. The work of many of the popular movements and voluntary associations is recognized by direct financial support from national and local governments. Established political parties also receive funding from the State and from county and municipal councils at a uniform rate per seat won. These subsidies form the main sources of party political funds. The press is also subsidized from public funds.

A conservative society and a serious shortage of capital ensured a relatively slow and peaceful adaptation to the concepts of democracy, co-operation and secularization. By the mid-twentieth century the Scandinavians had achieved more stable democracies than the French, more representative parliamentary systems and comprehensive co-operative movements than the British and more humane bureaucracies than the Germans. The replacement of industrial strife by negotiation widened the appeal of the social-democratic parties and ushered in long periods of social-democratic government (Figure 1.4). Competition between the social democrats (whose original electoral base, the industrial working class, is in numerical decline) and the centre and right parties for the votes of the expanding groups – service-industry workers and pensioners – has discouraged radical departures from existing consensus by either left or right when in government. With the support of the business community and control of the majority of Scandinavian newspapers, the centre and right-wing parties mount a lively criticism of social-democratic aspirations and policies.

1.2.3 *Current social policies and political debate*

The so-called 'Nordic Model' Welfare State is characteristically comprehensive, involving income redistribution, full employment, regional redistribution and democratic decision-making at all levels of society. Welfare benefits are seen as rights and not as handouts for the needy. High levels of welfare and public-sector employment depend upon thriving market economies with healthy export sectors. Table 1.2 shows how public spending in Scandinavia has risen above the average proportion of GDP in the developed countries of the Organization for Economic

Table 1.2   The public sector in Scandinavia

	Public spending as a % of GDP				% employed in public sector		
	1960	1975	1980	1987	1975	1980	1986
Denmark	29	48	56	57	24	28	29
Norway	30	48	51	53	19	22	23
Sweden	31	49	62	60	26	31	33
OECD	29	38	39	40	15	15	15

Source: Nordic Council of Ministers (1989).

Co-operation and Development (OECD). The public sector also employs a substantially higher proportion of the working population than in the average OECD country (Table 1.2).

The compromises that defined the roles of the public and private sectors, generally avoiding State ownership of industry but providing ways of distributing a share of rising prosperity to the employees, were established during the 1920s and 1930s. They have retained broad consensual support ever since, for Scandinavian governments have been reluctant to influence the commercial judgements of firms unless these appear to have serious social consequences. Unemployment arising from rationalization has been mitigated by national subsidies for the retraining and relocation of workers and by regional policies (Chapter 5, sections 5.1, 5.5). The so-called 'Scandinavian Model' of wage negotiation rests upon the view that wages in these small countries are determined by world market conditions in the export industries and the growth of productivity. Wages in those economic sectors that are 'sheltered' from foreign competition, notably the services and agriculture, should ultimately be determined by wages in the sectors 'exposed' to foreign competition. Such a model requires a high degree of centralized wage negotiation. Union wage-solidarity policies and the reduction of differentials originally involved the equalization of wages for *similar categories* of skill — equal pay for equal work — rather than the narrowing of wage differentials *between* skill categories. Solidaristic policies are believed to accelerate industrial change by squeezing the profit margins of the less efficient firms, leaving market forces and corporate choice to determine the direction of change.

The balance of parties and interests in each of the Scandinavian countries ensures that public debate focuses on incremental changes. Proposals for radical change in the Nordic Model are confined to relatively small, radical, left-wing parties and populist low-tax parties, which have emerged in Denmark and Norway during the last twenty years.

The relatively high levels of Scandinavian taxation are shown in Table 1.3. The tax systems of the three countries are by no means uniform. Denmark relies more heavily on income tax and less on social contributions than Norway and Sweden. National income taxes are progressive but local taxes may be levied as a fixed proportion of all incomes. Value added taxes (VAT) are relatively high and there is an increasing tendency to gain more revenue from non-progressive taxes. The effects of high taxes on profits are mitigated by generous depreciation allowances. Tax systems favour increases in productivity that come from substituting capital equipment for labour.

It is now widely accepted that changes are necessary in order to bring tax regimes more in line with those of competitor industrial countries by reducing national income tax, rationalizing the complex system of deductions and raising taxes on capital. In Norway, the highest marginal income-tax rate has already been reduced from 74 per cent in 1986 and 62 per cent in 1989 and the Danish government intends to reduce corporation taxes by 1994. The Swedish government plans to abolish national income tax for people earning less than 180,000 SKr (about £18,000, US$30,000), leaving them liable only for local income tax at 31 per cent. Higher wage earners would pay a national income tax at 20 per cent. Corporation tax will be reduced but VAT and petrol taxes raised and many exemptions removed so that the contribution of taxes to GDP will remain at about 56 per cent.

The 'Nordic Model' Welfare State (Kesselman and Krieger, 1987) reached the height of its development and consensual support during the 1960s, when living standards were rising steadily and Scandinavian products found ready markets at home and abroad. The international economic crises of the 1970s and increasing competition from Japan and Third World countries reduced the overseas sales of some Scandinavian goods and accentuated the differences between manufacturing, mining and some agricultural production, which relied heavily on export earnings, and the 'sheltered' industries, notably the services, which produced only

Table 1.3   The percentage share of tax contributions to total revenue, 1987

	Denmark	Norway	Sweden
Income tax	56	36	44
Social contributions	3	22	26
Indirect taxes	35	39	29
Property taxes	5	2	3

Source: Nordic Council of Ministers (1989).

for home markets. The interest of different groups of producers and consumers diverged. Central wage bargaining suffered a partial break-down. Coalition governments based on centre and right parties became more frequent.

At the outset of the present decade, the political questions of the 1990s appear to revolve around the extent to which the Scandinavian countries will wish to align their social and economic policies with those of the EC countries in order to compete in the wider European market, or to accept a slower economic growth in order to preserve their distinctive social consensus.

The political systems of Scandinavia are structured to encourage shrewd appraisal, caution and conservative attitudes towards change. Election by proportional representation allows all citizens an equal influence on the formation of governments and local councils. While small parties may represent only limited sectional or regional interests they can influence national policies as prospective coalition partners if no single party has an overall majority. In these circumstances party leaders have strong incentives to compromise with each other and to propose incremental rather than radical change.

The political spectrum is similar but not identical in the three countries, for there are more parties in the Danish and Norwegian parliaments than in Sweden. The most important distinction lies between parties of the right and centre (Progress, Moderate, Conservative, Liberal, Centre, Christian) and those of the left (Social Democrats, Socialists and Communists). The Greens stand somewhat outside the right–left spectrum.

The small Progress parties of Denmark and Norway advocate economic liberalism and social conformity, lower taxation and restrictions on im-migration. Professional and business interests are represented by Con-servative and Liberal parties. The Centre (previously Farmers) and Christian Peoples parties have latterly sought to attract urban voters by campaigning for a better environment and a more balanced regional development while opposing big business, centralized union power and liberal abortion laws.

Social Democractic parties traditionally represent the industrial working class and the trades unions but have also attracted many professional workers with Marxist or reformist interests. After just one electoral defeat in 1976, the Swedish Social Democrats adopted a pragmatic approach to economic development and defence. Other left-wing parties are now reformist rather than revolutionary and ideologically rather than class based. They have given essential parliamentary support to minority Social Democratic governments in recent years. In 1988 the Greens made their first appearance in a Scandinavian parliament by winning twenty seats in Sweden. Their support is largely drawn from young, well-educated city dwellers often in public-sector employment.

Left and centre-right parties are rather evenly balanced in Scandinavian parliaments but the parties on the right have found it more difficult to devise a common programme than those on the left. In these circumstances the Social Democrats have, to a considerable extent, set the field for political debate since the mid-1930s. Their so-called 'middle way' was a compromise whereby the working classes recognized the market as the most efficient way to organize production, and businessmen (rather reluctantly) accepted government interventions designed to support equal opportunity and to resolve other social problems.

Figure 1.4 shows which parties have provided the Scandinavian governments during the last thirty years. Social Democrats governed Sweden, often in alliance with smaller parties, from 1933 to 1976 and from 1982 to the present, although they only held an absolute majority of seats in 1941–4 and 1969–70. In Denmark and Norway long periods of Social Democratic rule gave way first to Social-Democratic-led coalitions in the 1960s and later to an alternation of left and centre-right coalition governments.

During the 1980s, Scandinavian right and centre parties (other than the Progress parties) showed no desire to roll back the Welfare State. Social Democrats reacted pragmatically to changing international circumstances, gradually giving greater support to EC membership. By 1990 the Swedish Social Democrats accepted that the maintenance of stable prices for their goods on world markets was more important than retaining virtually full employment.

1.3   Post-war prosperity and economic development

Table 1.4 shows the growth of population and employment in Scandinavia since 1960. While the population only increased by 14 per cent between 1960 and 1987, the workforce grew by 2.4 million (37 per cent) as large numbers of women became part-time or full-time employees. The great majority of women found work in the service sector (including utilities), which more than doubled in size between 1950 and 1989 (Figure 3.4, p. 103), and now dominates the occupational structure. Employment in the manufacturing industries (which include the construction industry) remained fairly stable until the 1980s, when it fell sharply. The agricultural population of Scandinavia halved. Economic growth (Figure 1.5) has been roughly comparable to that of West Germany. GDP per head was similar to that of the UK in 1950 but was one third higher by 1989. The rate of economic growth varied between the three countries (Table 1.5), with the Norwegian economy growing particularly rapidly in the 1970s during the initial development of North Sea oil.

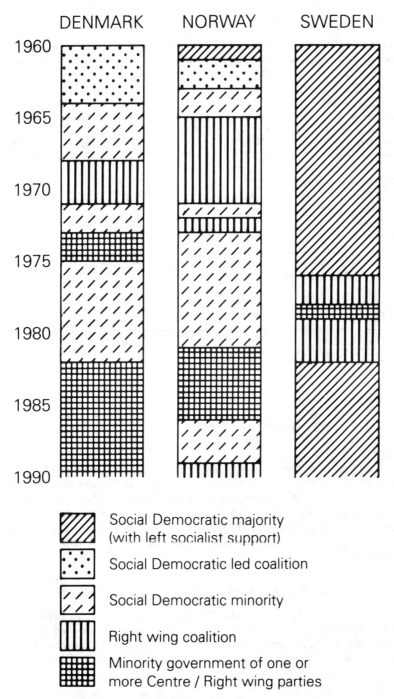

Figure 1.4 Scandinavian governments, 1960–90

Table 1.4 Population and employment, 1960−88 (forecast for 2000)

	1960	1970	1980	1988	(2000)
Population (000s)					
Denmark	4,565	4,951	5,100	5,130	(5,300)
Norway	3,595	3,888	4,092	4,221	(4,300)
Sweden	7,498	8,081	8,318	8,459	(8,300)
Scandinavia	15,678	16,920	17,510	17,810	(17,900)
Employment (000s)					
Denmark	2,001	2,310	2,451	2,686	
Norway	1,380	1,462	1,913	2,114	
Sweden	3,233	3,413	4,232	4,399	
Scandinavia	6,614	7,185	8,596	9,199	

Sources: National censuses; Nordic Council of Ministers (1989); *Yearbook of Nordic Statistics* (1988 and 1989−90).

Table 1.5 Percentage annual change in GDP, 1970−89

	1970−80	1980−5	1989
Denmark	2.3	2.5	0.75
Norway	4.7	3.4	1.80
Sweden	2.0	1.8	1.70

Source: Nordic Council of Ministers (1989).

The causes of these changes and their varying regional effects will be discussed in more detail in Chapters 2−5. The remainder of this section describes the related political and policy changes within each country. The period from 1960 to 1990 has been rather arbitrarily divided into a period of rising prosperity (1960−72) followed by setbacks from 1973 to 1980 (section 1.3.1) and a cautious resumption of growth since 1980 (section 1.3.2).

1.3.1 From prosperity in the 1960s to crises in the 1970s

The end of the Second World War found Scandinavia in better shape than Western Europe, for its towns and infrastructure had not been seriously damaged (apart from Bornholm and Arctic Norway) and resistance to foreign occupation and external threats had strengthened social

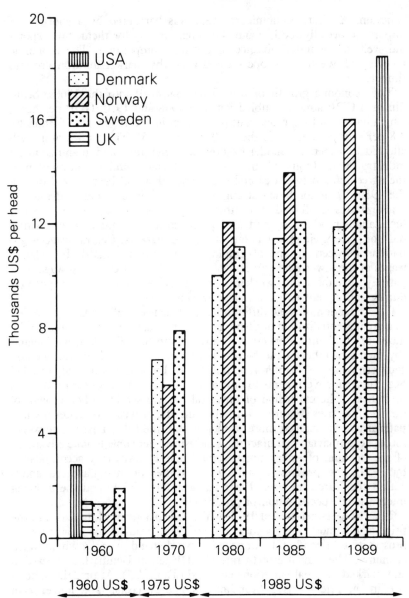

Figure 1.5 GDP per head, 1960–89

cohesion. At first, economic recovery was hampered by a shortage of imports (especially fodder) and the dollars to pay for them, but exports did well in the initial absence of German competition. The economic recovery of Western Europe created a nearby market for iron ore and timber.

The economic growth of the 1950s continued into the 1960s. Scandinavian GDP almost doubled between 1948 and 1970. GDP per head, which had risen by 2.6 per cent per annum in the 1950s, rose further by 3.8 per cent per annum in the 1960s (Figure 1.5). These rates of growth allowed considerable modernization of agriculture and manufacturing industry, a steady growth in service employment and a continuation of the agreements between capital and labour that had been forged during the 1930s. The combined strength of the employers' and trades-union organizations reinforced each other. Employers and unions both sought high labour productivity and were prepared to settle for wage levels that did not price their products out of foreign markets. Central wage negotiations between groups of employers and unions raised the relative wages of the lower-paid and female workers but failed to stop wage drift entirely since the skilled workers were often able to improve their position during subsequent bargaining at company level.

The reduction of wage differentials and revisions of the tax system led to a greater equalization of disposable income that, in turn, facilitated the mobility of labour. Workers were drawn into Scandinavia from Finland (by then a member of the Nordic labour market), southern Europe and southern Asia (see Chapter 4, section 4.1.1). Increasing prosperity enabled Scandinavian governments to pursue simultaneous policies for production growth and the expansion of universal welfare services. The growth of service industries (Figure 3.4, p. 103) and the provision of maternity and paternity leave enabled more women to join the full- or part-time workforce. Scandinavian manufacturing industries were able to take advantage of the opening of international capital markets (virtually accomplished by 1959), the progressive removal of duties on manufactured goods within the European Free Trade Association (EFTA) and the growing international specialization of production.

The Arab–Israeli war of 1973, which led to a series of increases in the price of oil, most notably in 1973 and 1978, brought the steady rise in prosperity to an end and dampened down demand over the whole world economy. The annual growth rate of GDP fell in Denmark and Sweden and marked national variations emerged (Table 1.5). At first the sudden rise in oil prices raised Scandinavian energy costs. The longer-term effects were not felt until 1975, when West European economies, now well into recession, reduced their orders for iron ore, timber and the products of the Scandinavian engineering industries. The increase in oil prices reinforced two other unfavourable economic trends of the 1970s: deliveries of iron ore and timber from the Third World were arriving at West European ports at lower prices than Scandinavians could offer; and the Japanese now became vigorous competitors in the price and quality of their machine tools, domestic hardware and other advanced products.

At first the Scandinavian governments treated the changed circumstances as a temporary recession. They stimulated their economies in the hope of riding out the storm while continuing long-term policies that gave the maintenance of high and stable employment priority over economic growth. The deceleration of economic growth soon threatened the welfare consensus and the centralized wage-negotiation systems established forty years previously. The interests of workers in manufacturing and service industries diverged and the efficiency of centralized decision-making was increasingly questioned. Public-sector employment continued to expand. In Sweden taxes accounted for 40 per cent of GDP in 1970 but 51 per cent in 1983, by which time they were the highest in all the OECD countries. Although economic growth was slower during the 1970s and there was less wealth to share, the aspirations of consumers rose rapidly as a new generation took to the roads in their private cars, saved time with new domestic appliances and travelled abroad in larger numbers.

Sweden felt the worst effects of the recession because of its reliance on imports of oil and exports of manufactured goods. Inflation at 10 per cent or more almost every year during the 1970s encouraged wage increases in manufacturing industry that, by the mid-1970s, were pricing Swedish goods out of world markets. Profits fell from 30 per cent of processing costs during the 1950s and 1960s to 15 per cent in the 1970s, but the share of wages rose rapidly from 60 per cent to 85 per cent.

The Social Democratic government, shunning direct intervention in wage negotiations, offered the trades unions a greater control over industrial investment and location through the Co-Determination Act, which appointed workers' representatives to the boards of companies and a proposal for 'wage-earner funds' whereby a proportion of company profits would be used to buy shares on behalf of the workforce. The fear that wage-earner funds would enable the unions and the State to gain control of large sections of the economy, together with increasing dissatisfaction with the government's handling of the developing economic crisis, led to the defeat of the Social Democrats in the 1976 election. The incoming centre-right coalition government devalued the krona, raised VAT, imposed cuts in public spending and increased subsidies to the ailing textile and shipbuilding industries. Subsidies to industry rose from one billion Skr in 1975 to 17 billion in 1982 but real wages fell by 9 per cent. Subsidies retarded the transfer of resources from the less to the more internationally competitive industries and supported a further rise in wage costs. In 1980, major industrial conflicts brought about a rapid wage inflation followed by further devaluation of the krona in 1981.

The Norwegian Labour government relied upon its oil resources and prospective revenues to ride out the economic troughs of the 1970s. Opposition to oil development was still voiced by many environmentalists, traditionalists and fishermen, and by the Christian Peoples, Centre and Socialist Left political parties. Government policy for oil was one of relatively slow extraction, so that existing manufacturing industries were not destroyed by an oil-induced inflation or by a rapid rise in the value of the krone. It was intended to use a substantial part of the oil revenue to invest in new manufacturing industries that would diversify the economy as oil revenues diminished in the late 1990s – but oil revenues were also used to create new jobs in the welfare services and to retain manpower in agriculture and the fisheries. The balance between investment in 'new' jobs and the preservation of employment in 'old' jobs was difficult to maintain and the Norwegian economy in fact experienced expansion from 1973 until 1977, followed by austerity policies from 1977 until 1981.

Production rose significantly after 1975 until, in 1982, income from oil and gas production accounted for 18 per cent of government revenues and 32 per cent of export earnings. However, the oil industry, including platform building and support services, only employed 3 per cent of the labour force.

During the late 1970s there was a growing deficit in the Norwegian balance of payments as a result of expansionary economic policies, heavy investment in oil-related industries and the loss of market share at home and abroad by the non-oil industries. Oil revenues were used to protect the rest of the economy against job losses and lower production. Norway increased its borrowing and took the opportunity to catch up and surpass the traditionally higher living standards and welfare benefits enjoyed by the Swedes. However, labour costs rose steeply and Norway soon became one of the largest debtor nations in the industrial world. Norway benefited, however, from the second oil price rise in 1978.

Public-service employment grew rapidly. National and local government accounted for 85 per cent of all new jobs between 1977 and 1981. Although inflation remained low and unemployment fell to 1.4 per cent, manufacturing industries outside the oil sector hardly grew at all between 1975 and 1982. Determined to maintain a high level of employment, Norwegian governments protected their agriculture at relatively high price levels, raising farmers' income by 50 per cent and also subsidized manufacturing firms. By 1979 the government was carrying 20 per cent of the wage bill of the shipyards. These policies gave rise to larger and larger deficits and, although patently failing to meet their objectives when world production failed to rise again in the late 1970s, were continued into the 1980s. Low property taxes and the offsetting of most personal interest payments against income encouraged people to buy housing and consumer durables (often imported) rather than to save.

Devaluation, credit controls, public spending cuts and a wage freeze were imposed by a Labour government in 1978. Wage settlements reflected the desire to protect workers from the worst effects of inflation and to spread the benefits of the rapidly burgeoning oil economy. However, the lifting of wage and price controls late in 1979 led to a further overheating of the economy and a loss of ground in export markets. A wage and price freeze was reimposed in 1981 but, by 1982, wage costs in Norway were higher than in all its European competitors and second only to those in the USA. Norway had lost one third of its manufacturing export markets between 1970 and 1981.

In Denmark, general economic trends during the post-war period towards a 'post-industrial' economy and the aspirations of the people for better social services, pensions, health care and more travel paralleled those in Norway and Sweden (Figures 1.5 and 3.4, p. 103; Tables 1.4 and 1.5). The Danish economy, lacking industrial raw materials until the development of North Sea oil and gas in the late 1980s, had traditionally relied upon agricultural exports to pay for imported industrial raw materials, fertilizers and manufactured goods. Since other EFTA countries did not freely open their markets to the more efficient Danish farmers, increases in productivity and specialization on Danish farms did not find sufficiently remunerative outlets for their products. Agricultural production was subsidized in Denmark from 1958 until entry to the EEC in 1973 brought the benefits of the Common Agricultural Policy to Danish farmers. Most Danish farms were small by West European standards but productivity was high on the larger holdings. The closure or amalgamation of the less profitable, smaller farms gradually released labour for employment in manufacturing and services. There was a rapid expansion of manufacturing industry during the late 1950s and 1960s, which depended as much upon Danish design flair and entrepreneurial skill as on domestic production and imported raw materials. Manufacture replaced agriculture and food processing as the dominant element in the economy.

Many of the factories and workshops were founded in rural areas, most notably in western Jutland, where new textile, clothing and furniture factories provided full- and part-time work for farming families and enabled others to abandon farming altogether (Clout, 1975). Bang & Olufsen is perhaps the best known of these. The development of computers enabled the travel agency, Tjæreborg, founded by a local parson, to bring employment to his village. Some factories supplied components to larger firms (often in Sweden) that were already well established in foreign markets. There was more international integration of Danish manufacturing industry although not on the scale of comparable Organization for Economic Co-operation and Development countries (OECD, 1989–1990).

Denmark suffered more markedly than Norway and Sweden from the economic recession of the 1970s and recovered more slowly. The Danish economy was characterized by low growth and investment, high inflation and unemployment rates well above those of Norway and Sweden. The Danish external account, which had almost balanced in 1972, deteriorated during the late 1970s, forcing a series of devaluations of the krone totalling 20 per cent between 1979 and 1981. This was, to some extent, because the expansion of the Danish economy and living standards during the 1960s had been partially funded by extensive borrowing abroad. Many of these loans had facilitated the production of goods and services that were sheltered from foreign competition. The repayment of interest on these loans in the 1970s and 1980s (eventually amounting to 4 per cent of GDP) was a continuing burden on the Danish economy and contributed to its sluggish growth. Since the first oil crisis of 1973, the annual growth of Danish GDP has been consistently 0.5 per cent below the OECD average. It must be appreciated, however, that services, which may improve the quality of life, are not included in these GDP calculations.

These economic problems weakened voter support for the main Danish political parties and led to a marked rise in the vote for the Progress Party in 1973. The parties of the right and centre experienced considerable fluctuations in voter support. A Social Democratic minority government from 1975 until 1982 undertook a series of tax increases and incomes policies in its attempts to reduce the balance-of-payments deficit.

1.3.2   The 1980s – policies to sustain economic development

During the 1980s Scandinavian manufacturing industries adapted to changes brought about in the economies of the developed countries by the economic crises of the 1970s, including shorter life-cycles for products, less standardization, smaller production runs, a greater exchange of components between factories, just-in-time delivery, new information technology, rapid adjustment to signals from the market and greater attention to research & development. All these changes required flexibility in the provision of both capital and labour. Fortunately, Norwegian (and later Danish) oil and gas provided new sources of energy and exports. The world timber market also improved.

Differences in the economic structures of the three countries – the growing significance of oil for Norway, of manufacturing export industries for Sweden and balance-of-payments problems for Denmark — led to marked divergencies in the economic policies of the three Scandinavian states. The political balance was also changing. The days of Social Democratic majority government were long past in Norway and Denmark but the left, although no longer able to win a majority of votes, was still dominated by the Labour Party in each country. On the right of the political spectrum, considerable divergencies of view between the Conservatives and the several centre parties led to a series of short-lived minority and coalition governments in both countries (Figure 1.4) which could only muster sufficient political support for short-term reactive policies.

In Sweden, however, the Social Democrats returned to power in 1982 after six years of government by centre-right coalitions. Production in the internationally competitive manufacturing industries was hardly above 1972 levels, and Sweden's share of world markets had fallen by 25 per cent. Under the determined leadership of Olof Palme, the Swedish Social Democrats set off on the so-called 'third way', rejecting both inflationary economic expansion and retrenchment with associated unemployment in favour of using the capitalist economy to deliver maximum output, and the public sector — the largest in any industrialized country — to redistribute the wealth created.

A major investment programme was launched to save energy (through district heating and other measures) and to develop domestic energy resources. By 1988 energy demand had been reduced to 1973 levels. While 78 per cent of Swedish energy had been imported in 1973, only 52 per cent was imported in 1988. There was major investment in road building and in the modernization of the railway and telecommunications networks. The industrial policy of the Social Democrats strongly supported research, development and new technology. At the same time industrial expenditure on research & development rose to 10 per cent of total costs in the mid-1980s — about the same ratio as in West Germany and Japan. The krona was devalued by 16 per cent and the trades unions persuaded not to seek compensation for the resulting increase in living costs. Devaluation was followed by a tight fiscal policy and an attempt to reduce wage differentials as much as possible. Arguing that real wages depend on real jobs, it was considered better to push workers out of declining industries than to buy them jobs in these industries through State subsidies.

The spread between the highest and lowest wages in manufacturing industry, which had been 30 per cent in the late 1960s, narrowed to 15 per cent by the mid-1980s. Low wage differentials made it easier for the unemployed to find work in other industries and firms. Three per cent of Swedish GNP was devoted to measures designed to reduce unemployment. Labour exchanges provided comprehensive information about new jobs and there was an extensive retraining programme. In 1987, 85 per cent of the Swedish unemployed were on skill training or other educational programmes compared to 32 per cent in Norway, 19 per cent in Denmark and 3 per cent in Britain. Relocation grants were also expanded. Unemployment benefit is withdrawn from workers who refuse to take up reasonable job offers or places on retraining schemes within ten months. With 4 per cent of the labour force normally on job creation or training schemes, Sweden created a highly flexible labour market in terms of its ability to cope with economic shocks. Unemployment never exceeded 3.5 per cent throughout the 1980s. The wage-earner funds, invested in Swedish firms, together with tax-free mutual funds, raised the level of share ownership to 40 per cent of the Swedish population by 1990 (compared with about 20 per cent in Britain and the USA).

Government policies were soon reinforced by improvements in world trade and economic activity. Oil prices were generally lower and forest-product prices higher than in the 1970s. Between 1983 and 1985 exports rose by 17 per cent, manufacturing production by 19 per cent and GNP by 8 per cent. Although world markets for forest, mining and steel products expanded rather slowly during the 1980s, the Swedish share increased significantly (OECD, 1988−9).

During the years of economic recovery there was a partial break-down in consensus politics. Although workers had shown that they generally preferred more pay in their pockets to a stake in the owner-ship of industry through wage-earner funds controlled by trades unions, the government enacted a modified version of the scheme in 1983. Wage demands from industrial and public-sector workers threatened both government counter-inflation policy and the success of Swedish exports. The increase in Swedish hourly wage costs in 1984 was double the average for OECD countries and the government imposed a price freeze. The power of the industrial employers and trades unions had been weakened by the growth of service industries and State employment, where most workers were members of unions outside the industrial workers' organization (LO). As in the other Scandinavian countries, almost all the new jobs were created in the public-sector services. The Saltsjöbaden Agreements on wage bargaining, which had lasted since 1936, were abandoned in 1986 (although partially re-instated in 1989). Unions in manufacturing industries agreed to some substitution of job security and better redundancy payments for large pay packets but opposed the reduction of differentials between skilled and unskilled labour. By the late 1980s, centrally negotiated wage settlements no longer concentrated on the average wage for each industry but on the base lines for subsequent local wage negotiations. Increasingly, pay packets reflected recognition of individual output and local skill shortages but, in a reversal of the original Scandinavian Model, wage leadership passed from the 'exposed' to the 'sheltered' sectors of the economy.

By the end of 1985 the government had ended all subsidies to manufacturing industries and most of the Swedish shipyards had closed down. These policies were supported by the voters in the general election of 1988 but the emergence of the Green Party, with twenty seats in the Swedish parliament and control of the political balance in forty municipal councils, heralded new items for the political agenda. In 1990, the Social Democratic government reacted to the deteriorating international competitiveness of the Swedish economy by declaring their intention to apply for EC membership, cutting employment in the public sector, postponing the planned closure of nuclear power stations and giving the control of inflation priority over the maintenance of full employment − a reversal of policies they had pursued since 1932.

In Norway the growing oil revenues buoyed up the economy. By 1981, oil revenues contributed 15 per cent of GDP (as much as the whole of manufacturing industry) but only employed 2 per cent of the workforce. Oil prosperity attracted foreign capital and allowed the continuation of subsidies to manufacturing industry and agriculture but, by retaining a relatively high exchange rate for the Norwegian krone, hampered the exports of the rest of manufacturing industry. The alternation of economic expansion (1984−6) and austerity policies (1986−9) continued, as did the redeployment of labour from the internationally competitive to the sheltered sectors of the economy.

The centre-right Willoch government of 1981 adopted Conservative tax-cutting policies but refrained from deregulating or privatizing State-owned industries in order to keep the support of the Centre Party. The intervention of government in the economy increased through continued subsidies to fishing, regional economies and uncompetitive industries. Interest rates were held as low as possible. By 1985, Norwegian domestic demand had revived sufficiently strongly enough to enable the manufacturing sector to improve output, productivity and investment. While the oil industry developed steadily in the late 1980s, the capital-intensive manufacturing industries − aluminium, chemicals and non-ferrous metals   prospered, but the other manufacturing industries were losing foreign markets as the whole Norwegian economy was becoming more dependent upon oil.

During 1986 the price of Norwegian oil fell from $30 to $8 per barrel, leaving Norway with a very large external trade deficit. Consumer prices rose by 9 per cent in the space of twelve months and the Progress Party joined Labour to bring down the Willoch government and to install a minority Labour administration led by Gro Harlem Brundtland (since the Norwegian constitution did not allow fresh elections) until 1989.

With the support of the right and centre parties, taxes were increased, consumer spending fell and the Norwegian krone was devalued, but the implementation of a shorter working week again raised Norwegian labour costs. In 1988 a further incomes policy was imposed although the price of oil had stabilized at $15 per barrel. Inflation fell from 10 per cent in 1986 to 4.5 per cent in 1989. During these drastic economic interventions support for the Social Democratic minority government declined. After the 1989 elections (notable for a marked increase in support for the radical, right-wing Progress Party), the centre and right parties had a majority of seats and the Conservative, Centre and Christian Democratic Parties formed a short-lived minority government under Jan Syse. Within this coalition, the Conservatives wished to apply to enter the EC but the Centre Party opposed such a move. In 1990, when, during nego-tiations about the proposed European Economic Space, the EC demanded the abolition of controls on foreign investment in Norway, the Centre Party left the coalition government, which then resigned. Gro Harlem Brundtland formed a minority Social Democratic government which favoured further negotiations with the EC.

Denmark recovered more slowly from the recession of the 1970s and suffered higher unemployment than either Norway or Sweden. Danish agricultural production was increasingly affected by the Common Agri-cultural Policy of the EC, which enabled increased agricultural exports. The exploitation of the Danish sector of the North Sea, which began in the late 1970s, has led to increasing supplies of domestic energy, which have markedly benefited the economy.

In 1982, when foreign debt had risen to 33 per cent of GDP, inflation had reached 9 per cent and unemployment 10 per cent, the incoming centre and right coalition government, under Poul Schlüter, adopted a new medium-term economic strategy. Local government spending was cut, public-sector wage increases restricted to 4 per cent and the indexation of many wages and social-security payments ended. Hourly earnings in manufacturing industry fell behind price increases between 1980 and 1985. Danish governments did not subsidize individual manufacturing industries, although generous tax concessions were given to private in-vestors in the shipbuilding industry. Meanwhile, the shift of employment into service industries, including government employment, proceeded apace. Service employment rose by 200,000 from 1979 to 1988, while manufacturing, construction and agricultural employment fell by 55,000. Further attempts to reduce public spending and raise revenues in 1984 led to a general election in which the Conservatives were confirmed in their policies by a large increase in their vote. In 1990, however, dis-agreements on taxation policy led to an election in which the Social Democrat and Social People's Parties won 47 per cent of the seats.

Another Schlüter minority government was formed relying upon Social Democratic support for its policies towards the EC.

Although the policies of Scandinavian governments had diverged during the 1980s, the end of the decade saw a convergence in their responses to the proposed single European market of 1993. The Nordic Council of Ministers now discourages policies of support for ailing industries and is trying to phase out government credit support for manufacturing industry except in respect of research & development and regional policies. They are also pressing for open markets in public procurement − a priority area in EFTA−EC co-operation. As a result, there have been significant developments in international trade in telecommunication and transport equipment, and in energy and water supply. The regulation of financial markets in Norway and Sweden is moving closer to the directives adopted within the EC.

1.4 Scandinavia in a changing world

1.4.1 North European integration and economic co-operation

Since the middle of the nineteenth century, growing numbers of Scandinavians have seen mutual co-operation as a means of strengthening their states, preserving their political and social heritage and safeguarding their interests through trade and joint action as a peace-seeking block. Co-operation has been sought in the fields of trade, labour markets, culture, social welfare, regional policy and international political initiatives. Similarity of languages and social structures has facilitated joint action on social and economic issues but political co-operation has been more difficult to achieve because of differing relations with non-Nordic nations and sectional interests within each country.

Once Norway and Iceland had achieved political independence and Finland had separated from Russia, the five nations began to forge a series of cultural and economic links. However, their individual experiences during the Second World War persuaded each country to make different alliances with neighbouring powers.

In social and cultural affairs, the Nordic Council, established in 1952, provides the main framework for co-operation and common research effort (Figure 1.6). The council consists of 87 elected representatives from the parliaments and (non-voting) nominated representatives of the governments of Denmark, Finland, Iceland, Norway and Sweden. It is an advisory body, concerned with all issues of common interest other than national defence and relations with individual non-Nordic countries. With the help of the council, the Scandinavian countries made considerable progress in harmonizing their social legislation. There is now a very large

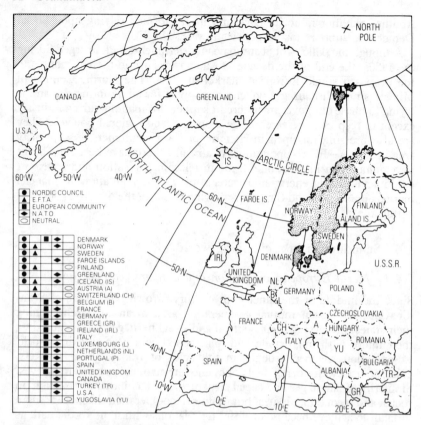

Figure 1.6 Scandinavia and its neighbours

measure of harmonization of family, commercial and transport law between the five countries. The 1982 Convention on Social Security allows all Nordic citizens to use the health and social-security systems of the country in which they are resident. The 1987 Language Convention allows them to use their native language in official correspondence even if resident in another Nordic country. The Nordic Council has also supported the establishment of three international planning regions − the Øresund conurbation, Nordkalott (the three northernmost counties of Norway and the northernmost counties of Sweden and Finland) and Arko (a small zone on the Norwegian−Swedish border at latitude 60° N). Each region has a different type of planning authority according to the scale of problems it faced.

The Nordic Council of Ministers, established in 1971, can take decisions within the limits of the Helsinki and subsequent agreements. Decisions must be unanimous, although ministers may abstain from voting.

The Nordic countries have gradually integrated some sectors of their economies and have also worked towards freer trade. Sectoral integration began with the establishment of the Scandinavian Airlines System (SAS) in 1951, comprising the national airlines of Denmark, Norway and Sweden. A combined railway-tariff system was agreed in 1953 (Finland joined later). The power grids of the four adjacent countries are interconnected through the Nordel agency. Negotiations are proceeding for a Nordic system of natural-gas pipelines.

The Common Labour Market, established in 1954, has helped to even out differences in the supply and demand for labour, thus reducing unemployment and dampening wage-led inflation during subsequent decades. A Nordic Investment Bank was set up in 1975. Although the Scandinavian banks have traditions of close mutual contact, differences in the structures of their capital markets have prevented any regular co-operation in monetary policy. The major Swedish devaluations of the 1980s were by no means welcomed by its Scandinavian neighbours. Although there is still no formal mechanism for monetary co-operation, the perceived need to keep in step with the liberalization of money markets within the EC is gradually allowing free-market forces a greater play in the capital market and aligning the monetary policies of the three countries. Denmark has been a member of the European Monetary System since 1979. The Nordic countries now work together in international exchange-rate policy and have had one joint representative on the board of the International Monetary Fund since the 1950s.

Between the Depression of the 1920s and the Second World War, all three Scandinavian economies suffered from the raising of trade barriers and international tariffs and quotas. The major manufacturing firms and the Danish farmers supported freer trade in order to develop their overseas markets. Unwilling to join the EEC in 1958, Denmark, Norway and Sweden, together with Britain, Austria and Portugal, set up EFTA in 1960. Finland became an associate member in 1961, and Iceland joined in 1970. Nordic economic and political co-operation during the 1970s and 1980s was, however, hampered by the adherence of Norway and Denmark to the North Atlantic Treaty Alliance (NATO) and Finland's non-aggression pacts with the Soviet Union. Proposals for a closer Nordic Economic Union (NORDEK) with a common external tariff and trade policy were abandoned in 1970 when Finland felt unable to join due to Soviet pressure. In 1972, Denmark narrowly voted to join the EEC in 1973. In Norway, however, the proposal to join was narrowly defeated in a national referendum. There was opposition from farming, fishing and some rural manufacturing interests who were heavily protected within the Norwegian market and felt unable to face wider competition within the Common Market and the sharing of fishing grounds.

Inter-Scandinavian trade remains one of the strongest economic bonds between the three countries, accounting for about one fifth of all Scandinavian trade. A new programme for the dismantling of barriers to inter-Nordic trade was adopted by the Nordic Council of Ministers in 1987.

The central programme for Nordic economic co-operation in 1989–92 is the Second Economic Action Plan. Assuming moderate economic growth in the early 1990s, as forecast by OECD, the Nordic Council of Ministers supports the phasing out of financial support for 'lame duck' industries and of trade-distorting government credits, favouring, instead, the liberalization of capital movements between the Nordic countries and the opening of the Nordic financial markets to foreign competition so that, eventually, Nordic financial legislation may be harmonized with that of the EC.

During the 1980s there was a considerable increase in take-overs and mergers between Scandinavian firms, notably in electrical engineering, electronics, machine tools and steel, which reinforced the position of central Sweden as the industrial heartland of Scandinavia.

The current problems for Nordic economic co-operation are seen by the Nordic Council (Nordic Council of Ministers, 1989) to be the fight against inflation, the encouragement of personal saving (which fell considerably during the 1980s), the development of greater efficiency in the public sector, the conservation of the environment, the further development of high and balanced growth within the Nordic internal market and the search for a common approach to the future single European market.

During the 1970s and 1980s, the larger businesses in Norway and Sweden, together with many Conservatives and Liberals, favoured eventual entry to the EC: but many Social Democrats, the Centre, Christian and Green Parties and most inhabitants of northern Norway and Sweden opposed entry. The political upheavals in central and eastern Europe that began in 1989, the re-unification of Germany in 1990 and the prospect of a single European market after 1992, have led to significant changes in the attitude of many Social Democrats and a more widespread belief that some form of European common market (including all Scandinavia) will be in place by 2000. A growing majority of Social Democrats now support entry, and the increasingly influential Norwegian right-wing Progress Party has moved from opposition to support (although opposition from the Centre Party brought down a Norwegian government on this issue in 1990). The growing integration of Denmark within the EC may well create problems for continuing Nordic co-operation unless Norway and Sweden harmonize their policies with those of the Community.

For decades, Swedish policy towards the EC and NATO has been determined by armed neutrality and the desire to do everything possible to support the independence of Finland. The rapidly changing political situation within the Soviet Union, and the demise of the Warsaw Pact, have reduced the significance of Swedish neutrality, at least in the short term. If the USSR were able to solve its daunting internal social and economic problems and reach a satisfactory *modus vivendi* with the Baltic republics, Swedish neutrality and Norwegian membership of NATO might assume less significance. Direr scenarios for the future of the USSR encourage Denmark and Norway to stay within NATO, while Sweden retains its neutral stance and keeps its powder dry.

In the meantime, Norway and Sweden propose to align their trade and business practices to those prevailing in the EC after 1992. During 1990 all the Nordic countries were involved in formal negotiations about a proposed European Economic Space (EES), which would include all the eighteen EFTA and EC countries by 1993 and might eventually attract central and east European countries as they dismantled their command economies. Within the EES, the EFTA countries would accept EC regulations on the movement of people, goods, services and capital, and EC policies on competition within the market and State aids to industry. While participating in EC research & development programmes and contributing to aid for its 'backward' regions, EFTA countries would not have to accept the EC Common Agricultural Policy or the dismantling of frontier controls. A special EC–EFTA court would oversee compliance with the rules of the EES, and its rulings would take precedence over national law. At the time of writing, negotiations over the EES are still in progress; however, in 1990 the Swedish government announced its intention to apply for membership of the EC. Because Norway is a member of NATO it has always been EC policy to give most favourable consideration to any Norwegian application for membership.

The dismantling of the command economies of central and eastern Europe seems likely to offer new opportunities for Scandinavian trade and investment. It is not yet clear how far the 'liberalization' of central and eastern Europe will encourage or weaken the trend to a much closer economic integration of the existing EC or whether Norway and Sweden will join the EC, form part of a peripheral group of non-members or achieve a relationship involving high levels of economic integration but political independence.

1.4.2 *Changing patterns of Scandinavian trade*

As highly developed but small industrialized nations, foreign trade plays an important part in the economies of all three Scandinavian countries. Only extensive foreign trading enables them to benefit from improvements in living standards made possible by capital-intensive production and modern technology, and to take advantage of economies of scale in production, investment, research, development and marketing. International trade also supplies an important competitive element, forcing ever higher productivity on native firms.

In the nineteenth century, Scandinavian exports of raw materials and food were balanced by imports of coal, manufactured products and luxury goods. Aware of the dangers of becoming peripheral suppliers of raw materials to the powerful industrial economies of Britain and Germany, Scandinavian governments encouraged the retention of national ownership of their resources and, by fostering widespread technical education, developed high-quality agricultural exports and built up a skilled industrial labour force. Manufactured products gradually replaced food and raw materials exports until, by 1987, as Figure 1.7 shows, they accounted for 70 per cent of all Scandinavian exports by value. The development of oil and gas fields in the North Sea enabled Norway and Denmark to widen their export repertoire. It is also notable that manufactured goods accounted for 80 per cent of the value of imports into the Scandinavian countries (including intra-Scandinavian trade) by 1987.

The restrictive international economic policies of the inter-war years held back the diversification of the Scandinavian economies but post-war Scandinavian governments, by lowering trade barriers and widening international markets, have achieved a considerable internationalization of their economies. Among specific export commodities, oil, oil products and gas from Norway were worth US$8.6 billion in 1987, Swedish exports of timber, pulp and paper were valued at US$8.0 billion, cars and trucks at US$6.8 billion and iron, steel and other metals at US$4.1 billion.

In 1960 Denmark, Norway and Sweden became founder members of EFTA, which comprised a number of countries on the geographical periphery of the EEC. EFTA is an industrial free-trade area with no common, external, trade barriers, no supranational authority and no joint economic policies. When Denmark (along with Britain) left EFTA to join the EEC in 1973, Norway and Sweden quickly negotiated reciprocal trading policies with the enlarged EEC and lifted tariff and import restrictions. Norway and Sweden have sought to harmonize their trading legislation and commercial policies with those of the EC.

Figure 1.7 shows that Scandinavian trade is overwhelmingly with the Developed World. EC countries (other than Denmark) are the main trading partners, accounting for half the value of the trade of Denmark and Norway and almost half that of Sweden in 1987. Inter-Scandinavian trade accounted for 22 per cent of Norwegian, 18 per cent of Danish and 15 per cent of Swedish foreign trade. The remaining European countries,

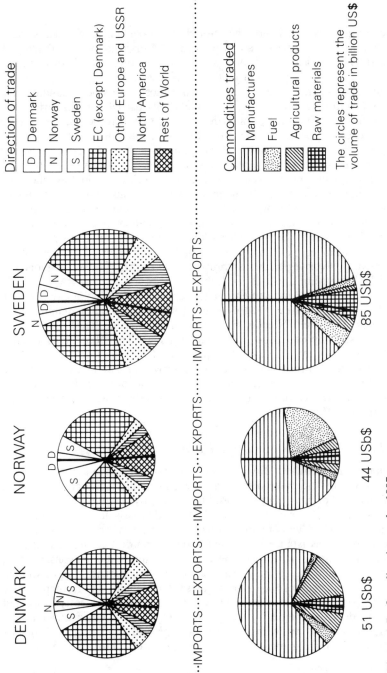

Figure 1.7 Scandinavian trade, 1987

including the Soviet Union, accounted for 14 per cent of Sweden's trade, 12 per cent of Denmark's and 8 per cent of Norwegian trade. Trade with North America accounted for 9 per cent of the foreign trade of Denmark and Sweden and 7 per cent of that of Norway.

Sweden, as the largest State with the most diversified economy, has long favoured a policy of free trade in industrial raw materials and manufactured products, importing goods that can be mass-produced more cheaply abroad. Over half of Sweden's international trade consists of 'inputs' − raw materials and components − but imports and exports of these input goods are equally balanced. Manufacturing industries are increasingly supplying special orders to the buyer's individual specification, exporting Swedish industrial technology and 'know-how' by using its relatively expensive labour force to assemble imported components for eventual export, and selling machine tools and manufacturing systems abroad. The size of the Swedish market relative to their own has encouraged Norwegian investment in Sweden, which accounts for 25 per cent of the turnover of Norwegian firms abroad and is the chief buyer of Norway's finished and semi-finished goods.

Oil is a significant element in the export trade of Norway, and, in 1987, oil exports were roughly equivalent to the value of manufactured exports. However, Norway has yet to find markets for all the oil and gas its self-imposed production quotas allow. The Norwegian electro-metallurgical industries export 75 per cent of their output. Denmark has a larger agricultural export sector than Norway or Sweden, but manufactured goods provide the greater part of the value of its trade. Denmark's trade with EC countries has become relatively more important since joining the Market in 1973.

1.4.3   Initiatives in the Third World

Scandinavian countries have given considerable financial assistance to the Third World and were disbursing the United Nations' target figure of 0.7 per cent of gross national product (GNP) by the mid-1970s. Norway has given over 1 per cent since 1982. All of this assistance is now given as grants − earlier loans to the poorest countries having been written off. Development assistance is targeted upon the poorest countries and gives special attention to sustainable development, environmental conservation, health care and education in rural areas and the contribution of women to economic progress. For these reasons economic aid is increasingly focused on Africa. Scandinavian governments have consistently supported independence movements, the political liberation of African countries from oppression by white minority groups and have protested against superpower infringement of the sovereignty of Third World nations.

Humanitarian assistance has been given consistently to national liberation movements both before and after the attainment of independence. Third World countries governed by what are perceived as oppressive and dictatorial regimes receive humanitarian aid but not economic assistance. Bilateral assistance is intended to allow the recipient countries to integrate external assistance with their own long-term development strategies.

Assistance began under the auspices of non-governmental and voluntary bodies but government development co-operation budgets were established during the 1960s. In the late 1970s government technical co-operation and research agencies were set up, including the Swedish Agency for Research Co-operation with Developing Countries (SAREC) and the Agency for International Technical and Economic Operation (BITS). These agencies operate in a wider range of developing countries than those receiving economic assistance. Under the Copenhagen Convention of 1981, much Nordic assistance to Third World countries is integrated into joint programmes.

As an example of Scandinavian aid, Sweden introduced balance-of-payment support programmes to ease the debt burden of the developing countries in 1985. Forty per cent of Swedish assistance is allocated to selected countries, 30 per cent is given through international agencies (most notably the United Nations Development Programme) and international development banks, and the remaining 30 per cent to other bilateral programmes, largely through the Swedish International Development Authority (SIDA), which is controlled by voluntary bodies and the political parties and concentrates upon health and educational assistance.

1.5 Geographical constraints and resources

An 'economic and social study' of Scandinavia must give some consideration to the physical background if only because modern civilization extends nearer the poles in Norway and northern Sweden than in most parts of the earth (apart from Finland, the Kola peninsula, Iceland and Alaska). In Scandinavia, as in Britain, the most difficult terrain and the poorest soils lie in the north and west. Since Scandinavians have made most contacts with the rest of the world through Denmark or across the Baltic and North Seas, the peripherality of the north and west is a function of both physical and human geography. A simple dichotomy between core and peripheral regions does not do justice to the complexity of the human and economic geography of Scandinavia nor to the variety of regional problems their governments have to tackle. In several areas climate, geology and the distribution of population interact to create multiple problems.

The human discomfort and economic costs imposed by the climate generally increase northwards. In Norway and northern Sweden, altitude reinforces climatic disadvantage westwards. Variations in the length of day are the most obvious features of a northerly latitude. The short winter days of central Norway and northern Sweden give way to almost permanent night at Kirkenes and Hammerfest in north Norway, where the sun at midwinter does not appear over the horizon for seven weeks. Natives of the north are accustomed to the dark winters and bright midsummers; southerners find adjustment more difficult and governments have compensated those who go to work in the far north ever since the eighteenth century. The long summer days, with the sun above the horizon for 18 hours in Oslo and Stockholm, help crops and tourists to make the most of the short summer-growth season (see Figure 2.1, p. 47).

The main differences in weather and climate within Scandinavia depend on the extent to which each region is open to penetration by the low pressure systems from the North Atlantic, which bring relatively high temperatures in winter but cause precipitation at all times of the year, or by air masses from Russia that cause warm and perhaps showery weather in summer but are invariably very cold in winter. These cold anticyclones encourage a great deal of healthy outdoor exercise for the well clothed and well fed but necessitate heavy insulation of buildings and/or high heating bills. Western Scandinavia is rescued from the low temperatures normal to the sixties and seventies latitudes by the transfer of warm water on the North Atlantic Drift, and warm air from the mid-Atlantic in low pressure systems moving into Scandinavia from the south west and south. These warming effects are restricted to the Norwegian fjords and coastal valleys. While Bergen (60°N) has no month with average temperatures below freezing, Oslo, on virtually the same latitude, has four.

The major contrasting physical regions of Scandinavia are shown in Figure 1.8. Historically, the Southern Lowlands of Denmark and Skåne and the discontinuous Central Lowlands between Oslo and Stockholm have provided the natural resources to support the largest populations and have broadly developed as the core regions of Scandinavia. The remaining physical regions – the Southern Uplands, Northern Plateaux and Western Mountains – have been peripheral.

Denmark, although wholly lowland, falls into two distinct physical regions. The islands and eastern Jutland have heavy but fertile clay soils. The soils of western Jutland, on the other hand, are formed from sandy outwash material from the edge of the last ice sheet and have been extensively reclaimed for agriculture only during the last 120 years. The coastal lowlands of Skåne, a complex of small plains and ridges benefiting

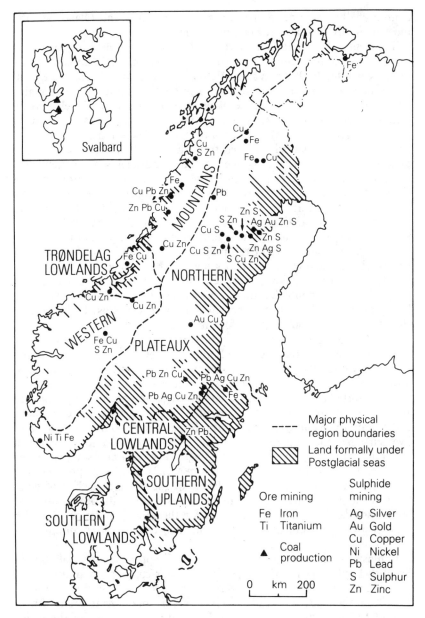

Figure 1.8 Major physical regions

from a chalky moraine, and the islands of Götland and Öland, are the most naturally favoured regions of Sweden.

The Central Lowlands extend from Oslofjord and Gothenburg eastwards to the Stockholm archipelago forming a series of small, discontinuous plains separated by Lakes Väner, Vätter, Hjalmar and Mälar, and by hill ridges that bear only thin, acid soils. The relative fertility of these plains owes something to the presence of pockets of sedimentary rocks with a significant lime content. After the melting of the ice sheets, the Central Lowlands were flooded by a series of postglacial lakes and seas in which a variety of clays and sands, eroded from the neighbouring uplands, were deposited. The highest coastline of the postglacial seas (which rises northward in relation to present-day sea level owing to the differential rising of the land after the removal of the weight of the ice) broadly separates the agriculturally productive from the agriculturally marginal land of Scandinavia. On the northern fringes of the Central Lowlands there are scattered deposits of iron ore, which were important historically in helping to locate many of the predecessors of the Swedish metal and engineering industries in the area known as Bergslagen.

The Southern Uplands of Sweden form a series of upland plains at 200–400 m between the Southern Lowlands and Lakes Väner and Vätter. Lying above the highest coastline of the postglacial seas, both soil and climate favour combinations of forestry and farming.

The Northern Plateaux slope gently eastwards from the Norwegian watershed towards the Gulf of Bothnia, where they merge into the Bothnian Lowlands. There are extensive plateaux at about 600 m. The lower reaches of the long valleys were flooded by postglacial lakes and seas that sorted out the loose material into strips and patches of potentially arable soil. Above the highest coastline of the postglacial seas (about 200 m around Oslofjord and in central Sweden and 300 m in the north of Sweden) the unsorted dead-ice moraine remains as a jumble of soil materials with very extensive peat bogs. The coniferous forest cover provides little in the way of nutrient materials and, with precipitation exceeding evaporation, the upper layers of the soil are leached of what little nutrient they may have. This land has historically been cultivated only when land has been insufficient for the local population or under very positive government action – and then only in close combination with forestry.

Extensive deposits of iron ore at Kiruna, Svappavaara and Gällivare in Swedish Lapland (with 35–60 per cent ferrous content) lay unused until basic linings for blast furnaces were invented and a railway was built in 1902 from the ice-free port of Narvik across the orefields to the Bothnian port of Luleå. Until the 1960s, the Lapland ores were one of the major sources of iron ore for the west European steel industries, 2,500 km to the south west. Of the production of 32 million tonnes in 1970, 86 per cent was exported.

Today the Scandinavian iron-mining industries exploit high-grade ores from mines at Kiruna and Gällivare in interior Lapland. Lower-grade ores are mined at Sydvaranger in northernmost Norway and in two smaller mines at Grängesberg and Dannemora in north-central Sweden. Almost 90 per cent of Lapland ore is exported through Narvik and Luleå, the remainder going to blast furnaces at Luleå and Öxelösund. Iron-ore output rose steadily until the 1970s, when technical developments in the steel industry (which favoured the low phosphorous ores only available from the Gällivare mines), the development of new Australian and South American ores (with lower costs of production and falling costs of transport) and the rationalization of the west European steel industry caused output to fall from 37 million tonnes in 1974 to 14 million tonnes in 1983. The Lapland mines, which required State subsidy from 1977 to 1982, developed pelletization and concentrated on their low phosphorous ores. Most of the smaller mines in Bergslagen were closed. Employment in the Scandinavian ore-mining industry fell to 6,000 in 1986 (forecast employment for the year 2000 is about 2,500), but production rose somewhat to 20 million tonnes in 1988.

Pyritic ores of silver, lead, zinc, gold and copper occur along the lower Skellefte valley (Figure 1.8). They are exploited by the Boliden company, which also produces sulphur and arsenic. Copper and lead are also mined in the vicinity. Laisvall, in western Lapland, has Europe's largest single source of lead. The Vielle Montagne mine in Närke smelts its ores abroad. These mines contribute up to 2 per cent of world production and 20–25 per cent of west and north European production. Europe's largest copper mine, producing 11 million tonnes annually, was opened recently at Aitik near Gällivare. Because of the range of minerals produced, changes in world market prices tend to balance each other and the metal-mining industry has not suffered the severe marketing problems of iron mining.

The high plateaux of western Norway rise very steeply from the coast to levels of 1,000–1,500 m, with extensive areas above the tree line. They are surmounted by mountains rising to 2,500 m. The plateaux fall stepwise to the south and east, scored by long open valleys linked by occasional gorges. The coastal cliffs are broken by deep, winding fjords along which the *strandflat* provides discontinuous strips of land for settlement. It is only in the Trondheim area and around Lake Mjøsa that moraines covering sedimentary rocks provide some lime to counteract the prevailing acidity of the thin upland soils.

There are iron-ore deposits near the Russian frontier at Sydvaranger and at Dunderland, near Mo i Rana. The ore is exported, as well as being used in Norway. There are also scattered copper deposits. Magnesium metals and alloys are extracted from sea water off Herøya in south-east Norway.

The most important recent mineral discoveries have been the extensive oil and gas fields in the North Sea. The internationally agreed meridian line of 1958 was found to have divided the main oil and gas fields between Britain, Norway and Denmark. The Statfjord and Frigg oilfields lie 170 km west of Bergen; Ekofisk is 330 km south west of Stavanger. After the oil crisis of 1973 output rose rapidly to reach 70 million tonnes in 1980. Exploration for further undersea oil wells is under way in the Norwegian Sea and towards the Barents Sea off the northern coast of Norway. Production has been limited by the difficulty of finding markets in Norway and abroad for the oil and gas. The exploitation of these mineral fuels has already led to very marked changes in the Norwegian economy, which have by no means run their course. Output is expected to fall towards 40 million tonnes per annum in the 1990s. The Danish sector of the North Sea has been more recently developed but is expected to supply half the energy needs of Denmark and to contribute to those of Sweden by the early 1990s. Oil and gas resources and their exploitation are discussed further in Chapter 3, section 3.1.

This chapter has shown how the Scandinavian economies have weathered the economic vicissitudes of the last thirty years and how, despite many disagreements, they have broadly maintained the ideals of the Welfare States established in the 1930s, despite a powerful international right-wing critique. Current living standards depend less on a wealth of natural resources than on political organization, education, social harmony and the broad consent of the people to maintain sophisticated economies and policies. The Scandinavian states have been generally successful in defending themselves against the political hegemony of their more powerful neighbours, but their living standards are becoming increasingly dependent upon their participation in international, especially European, markets. Further economic integration into Europe may require the acceptance of market rules that will make the maintenance of equal opportunity for all citizens and of all parts of Scandinavia more difficult to achieve. The price of participation in a more integrated European Community may be paid at a national level by the acceptance of regulations that are more suitable to the economies and policies of France, Germany and Italy. At the level of the firm, the removal of barriers to the acquisition of Scandinavian firms by foreign-based multinational companies may modify the profitable arrangements whereby Scandinavian-owned multinational firms, such as Electrolux, SKF and Volvo, undertake lower value-added operations abroad while keeping management and research & development sectors at home.

The next chapters look at the Scandinavian organization of agriculture, industry and the social services in more detail, and discuss how spatial and environmental conflicts of interest may be reconciled through their planning systems.

TWO

Resources and the Rural Economy

2.1 Agriculture and forestry

Scandinavia straddles the physical limits for cultivation and contains the most northerly cultivated areas in the world. The extent and type of farming is, not surprisingly, still strongly influenced by climate and soils. Scandinavia has the world's longest high-latitude growth season because of the combination of the long hours of summer sunlight and the warming effect from the south west of low-pressure, sub-tropical air systems and the North Atlantic ocean currents. The western uplands receive an annual precipitation of above 2,000 mm from this warm, moist air. Annual precipitation declines northwards and eastwards to under 500 mm as high-pressure continental air-masses become more dominant (and also the lee of the mountains), but this is usually sufficient for agriculture. Most of the agricultural lowlands receive between 500 mm and 750 mm precipitation per year.

Average July temperatures at sea level decline slowly northwards but sharply with altitude, so that Copenhagen (at 56°N), the Trøndelag lowlands (at 64°N) and the northern Bothnian lowlands (at 66°N) all average 15°C. Most of Scandinavia south of 68°N and below 500 m receives more than 800 day degrees of temperature above the 6°C threshold, where crop growth starts (Figure 2.1). This is sufficient to ripen the most popular grain crop, barley. Wheat, which requires 1,000 day degrees to ripen, can be grown at 64°N in Norway's Trøndelag lowlands and the mid-Bothnian lowlands of Sweden. Late frosts can occur at any time and are a hazard for agriculture throughout Scandinavia.

In winter, temperatures fall rapidly eastwards and northwards in the interior, as cold continental air increasingly dominates. Temperatures also fall with altitude. The nearly fresh-water Gulf of Bothnia freezes for four months and, in the northern interior, the intense winters last from October to May. The North Atlantic, North Sea, Skagerrak and Kattegat coasts remain ice free, however, and western coastal temperatures decline slowly northwards. On the western coast, Bergen at 60°N averages 2°C

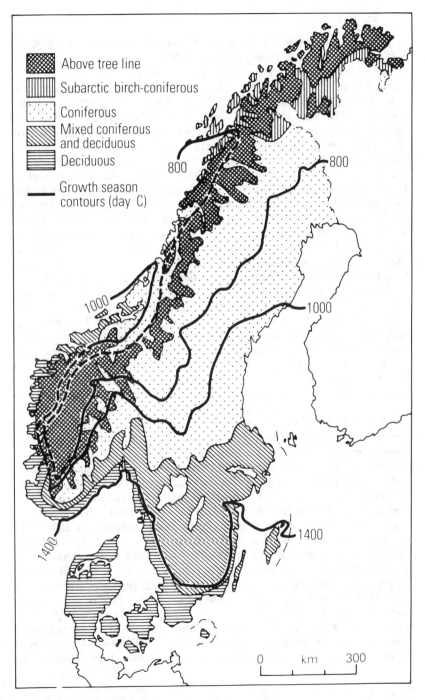

Figure 2.1 Natural vegetation and growth seasons

in January, and Tromsø at 69° N −4° C, whereas Oslo, also at 60° N but 300 km from the west coast, averages −5° C.

Soils are often thin, stony and of poor fertility, and are commonly formed from glacial materials. There are also large areas of bare rock. The richest soils are the relatively fertile boulder clays of east Jutland, the Danish islands and Skåne, derived from the cretaceous chalk and limestone rock base. Relatively good soils also developed on cambro-silurian limestones in parts of the central belt of Sweden, the islands of Öland and Gotland, the Trøndelag lowlands and neighbouring Dalarna, and the easily eroded cambro-silurian deposits stretching from the western Oslofjord to the Lake Mjøsa area. Elsewhere, especially in the mountains, soils are thin and poor and, in northern Norway and Sweden, are often covered with peat. They overlay the ancient, hard, crystalline granites and gneiss, which form most of Sweden and parts of Norway, and the folded and uplifted cambro-silurian deposits and harder precambrian sandstones that constitute the mountain backbone of Norway and Sweden. Other soils are formed from outwash deposits, as in west Jutland.

Forest cover is the natural vegetation response in most of Scandinavia (Figure 2.1). However, much of the upland area is above the tree line, which falls from 1,250 m in south Norway to 900 m in Trøndelag and only 650 m in north Norway, whilst some of the far north and mountain fringes have tundra vegetation. The permanent snow line averages 1,650 m in the south, falling to 650 m on the Finnmark coast. Norway's western and northern salt-water coastlines and adjacent islands are also treeless. Mixed deciduous forest naturally covered Denmark, Skåne, the coastal areas of west Sweden and parts of south and west Norway. Mixed coniferous and deciduous forest covered the rest of south Sweden and parts of south-east Norway and Trøndelag, whilst coniferous forest covered most of northern Sweden and much of Norway.

Most of the original forest cover has now been replaced by planted conifers or arable farming. Arable farming dominates Danish land use, covering 25,700 km² or over 60 per cent of the country (Table 2.1). Sweden has a similar area of arable farming (28,870 km²), but this is only 7 per cent of Sweden's area, and is mainly concentrated in much of the south west and parts of the central lowlands. Norway has only 8,940 km² of arable land, a mere 2.9 per cent of the total land area, located mainly in parts of the south east, Jæren near Stavanger, and Trøndelag. Coniferous forest largely dominates Swedish land use, 227,420 km² representing over 55 per cent of the total area. Norway's 66,600 km² of forest covers more than a fifth of the country, whilst Denmark has less than 5,000 km² of forest, but this covers a ninth of the land. Most of Scandinavia's forests contain numerous small pockets of farming and account for much of the small area of permanent pasture and meadow. Unproductive land

Table 2.1 Scandinavia: land use, 1988 (km^2)

	Arable		Permanent pasture and meadow		Forest		Unproductive		Total
Denmark	25,700	(60.6%)	2,170	(5.1%)	4,930	(11.6%)	9,590	(22.6%)	42,390
Norway	8,940	(2.9%)	1,020	(0.3%)	66,600	(21.7%)	230,250	(75.0%)	306,810
Sweden	28,870	(7.0%)	5,600	(1.4%)	227,420	(55.3%)	149,040	(36.3%)	410,930

Source: *Yearbook of Nordic Statistics* (1989–90).

covers three quarters of Norway, which is mainly land above the tree line, lakes, rivers and marshland, bare rock or steep slopes that are inaccessible for productive or urban use. More than a third of Sweden and a fifth of Denmark are also unproductive.

Traditionally, Scandinavian farming and forestry were often linked in a mainly subsistence dual economy; part-time food production was, largely, for farm consumption, and part-time forestry provided fuel, construction material and a cash export crop. Specialization, commercialization and concentration of forestry and farming have reduced this link and largely separated forestry jobs from farming employment.

Small, family-owned and run farms are the norm in Scandinavia, although the leasing of additional land from disused neighbouring farms is common in all three countries. In the last forty years, farms have increased in size by amalgamation. The number of farms has also been reduced by the abandonment, leasing or conversion to forestry of uneconomic farms, mostly in the settlement fringe zones, when farmers retire or die. This has caused a reduction in the area farmed in all three countries. Many *seters*, which provide natural mountain pasture for summer grazing, have become disused as transhumance has largely been abandoned (Bjørkvik, 1963). In Denmark the number of farms fell by more than half from 185,000 in 1951 to 84,000 in 1988, with an average arable area of 31 hectares − the second largest in the EC after the UK. Only Danish farms with over 50 hectares are increasing in number. Although Sweden's farms are slightly smaller, with an average 29 hectares of arable land, the number of farms declined by nearly two thirds from 282,000 in 1951 to only 101,000 in 1988, with only those over 30 hectares increasing in number. Norway has the smallest farms in Scandinavia, averaging 10 hectares of arable land, and the rationalization process is less advanced. Forty per cent of Norwegian farmers' income comes from outside agriculture. Norway's farms decreased by 40 per cent from 143,000 in 1949 to 86,000 in 1988, with only farms over 10 hectares of arable land increasing in number. The larger farms are found in Denmark, southern Sweden and southern Norway with size diminishing northwards.

Scandinavian farms are now highly mechanized. Tractors and combine harvesters had largely replaced horses and hired labour in Denmark and Sweden by 1970, and in Norway by 1986. This released surplus rural labour for migration to urban areas. There are now very few agricultural workers beyond farming families. Total employment in all primary activities (mainly agriculture) in 1988 was only 168,000 or 3.8 per cent in Sweden, 153,000 or 5.7 per cent in Denmark and 134,000 or 6.3 per cent in Norway (see Table 1.4, p. 20). However, the number of part-time farmers is now increasing. Half of Swedish farmers had non-farm income in 1986, in the main from urban jobs (Swedish Institute, 1988a). In

Norway, 54 per cent of farmers had a majority of non-farm income in 1988 and fewer than a quarter drew their income entirely from farming. Tourism provides farmers with another useful source of income from summer cottages, tourist huts, camping and farm holidays. Many new jobs in food processing have replaced jobs lost in food production (Törnqvist, 1986).

Chemical fertilizers are widely used in Scandinavia to increase soil fertility, as are insecticides, fungicides and herbicides, to increase crop yield, and growth regulators are used to increase animal growth. Growing concern for the environment has been heightened by algae growth and seal deaths in the sheltered waters of the Skaggerak, Kattegat and Baltic, both blamed on the run-off of chemical additives from farms. In all three countries the response was to reduce the use of fertilizers and pesticides during the 1980s. Meanwhile, the economic limits of grain cultivation have moved sharply southwards since the 1970s and many northern farmers have switched to hay growing for cattle fodder. Barley, for animal fodder, is the most common grain crop in Denmark, central and northern Sweden and the south-east and Trøndelag areas of Norway.

Scandinavian agriculture is dominated by livestock rearing, especially pigs and cattle. In Denmark and south Sweden pig and cattle rearing are most important, with over half the arable land growing grain for animal fodder. In the other arable areas cattle rearing predominates, with reindeer herding important in Lapland and sheep rearing in the west, north and eastern interior of Norway. Most food processing is by producer co-operatives, which produce meat and dairy products for the home market and, in Denmark's case, Lurpak butter, Danish bacon and Danish cheese for export, particularly to Britain and Germany. As transport has improved, processing has become increasingly concentrated to reap economies of scale. In Sweden, for example, the number of dairies declined from 1,000 in 1940 to 100 in 1980 (Törnqvist, 1986). Three quarters of Swedish farms contain forest land and upland, and northern Norway and Sweden are dominated by small and poor forest farms dependent upon forestry for much of their cash income. In coastal areas of Norway, the other traditional crofter-fishermen dual economy of part-time farming and fishing has also declined, with specialization producing a smaller number of jobs in commercial fishing, fish processing and farming (Coull, 1971). Many small farms have been abandoned as a result. Fruit farming is important on the shores of Sognefjord, whilst fur farming (fed on the waste from fish processing plants) is a modern way of linking farming and fishing.

Scandinavian agricultural policies have some common objectives, although Norwegian and Swedish agriculture are heavily subsidized, whilst Danish agriculture is much more commercial and export orientated and is subject to the rules of the EC's Common Agricultural Policy (CAP). CAP rules prevent Denmark, for example, from using import controls to protect home producers from cheaper food from the EC. All Scandinavian governments aim to make good-quality food available to consumers at reasonable prices and guarantee efficient family farms an income and living standard similar to that of industrial workers, mainly through regionally differentiated price support. This requires large subsidies in Sweden and Norway, costing the Swedish government, for example, 3,200 million SKr in 1985–6 for price support (mainly for milk) in addition to 378 million SKr in price support for northern agriculture.

As a neutral country, Sweden's main food production objective is to guarantee food supplies, even in war time or under blockade; this policy boosts total food production but at great cost. Norway, in contrast, has a low degree of self-sufficiency in food. Scandinavian agricultural policies also aim to protect the environment and to maintain employment and settlement in economically weak, usually remote, areas. In Norway and Sweden in the 1980s high prices to consumers and high-cost food surpluses, especially of meat and dairy products, stimulated calls for changes in policy. Future EC membership would require Norway and Sweden to remove most of its agricultural protection, which is why most farming areas voted heavily against membership in the 1972 Norwegian referendum, as did the Norwegian Farmers' Union in 1989. Von Würtemberg (1987) estimates that agricultural protection of $2,826 million in Norway and $4,218 m in Sweden in 1984–5 amounted to 37 per cent more in each country than the value added to the economy by agricultural production. In 1989 the Norwegian Farmers' Meat Marketing Association predicted that all Norwegian farmers would be unprofitable except for the major dairy farms of Norway's south-west coast, if Norway joined the EC.

Sweden's main natural resource is its massive 227,420 km^2 of forest, which covers over 55 per cent of the country, represents nearly 1 per cent of the world total and dominates Scandinavia's forests. Of Sweden's forest, 84 per cent is coniferous, mostly Norway spruce or Scots pine. Half of the forests are privately owned, 23 per cent by forest companies, 19 per cent by the State and 8 per cent by other public bodies, such as municipalities and the church (Table 2.2). Seventy per cent of State, or crown, forests are located in the two northernmost countries of Norrbotten and Västerbotten, where forestry is least profitable. Of company forests, 87 per cent are in the seven northernmost counties, with the largest area in Jämtland. Seven forest-products companies own 90 per cent of company forest, of which the largest, Svenska Cellulosa AB, owns 17,000 km^2 (Swedish Institute, 1988c). Over one fifth of forest land, including half of the private forest area, is managed in combined forestry and farming

Table 2.2 Scandinavian forestry ownership and production

	Forest area (km^2)	State	Other public	Private company	Other private	Net production 1988 (million m^3)
Denmark	4,930	30%	12%	12%	46%	1.9
Norway	66,600	10%	6%	4%	80%	11.1
Sweden	227,420	19%	8%	23%	50%	53.0

Source: *Yearbook of Nordic Statistics* (1989–90).

units where farming is still active. Half of the private forest owners, however, now live in urban areas. Private forests are most important in the central and southern counties where tree growth rates are the fastest.

The conditions for forest growth depend on local climate and soil conditions. The tree line falls from 700 m at 60° N to 400 m in northernmost Sweden. Gross forest growth declines from an annual average of 8 m^3 per hectare in the south to only 3 m^3 per hectare in the far north, with an average of 5 m^3. The growth cycle or rotation period for mature trees is 70 years in the far south to a height of 30 m, and a diameter of 30 cm, compared with 140 years, 15 m and 20 cm in the far north. Annual growth totals 90 million m^3 and of this about 65 million m^3 gross (53 million m^3 net of bark) was extracted in 1988, which was 10 per cent less than in the 1970s. Swedish forest stocks are, therefore, rising. Three quarters of the cut is from blanket felling and a quarter from thinning, 70 per cent is replanted from nursery stocks and the rest, mainly pine, regenerates naturally.

Since the 1960s, aerial dressing with nitrogen fertilizer has boosted forest yields, and 20,000 hectares are drained annually. Insect damage was a difficult problem in the 1970s and storms sometimes damage spruce forest, but fire is rarely a problem. In the 1980s, acid rain, mainly from Polish, German and British air pollution, emerged as a threat to Swedish forests, which suffered defoliation and increasingly acid soils.

Management plans that conserve timber stocks are used to run State forests, large company forests and some private forests. Timber extraction is now highly mechanized, with felling, limbing and length cutting mainly by harvesters, and debarking at the mills. Chain saws are still important for thinning, which occurs pre-commercially when trees reach 2–3 m in height and then from one to four times during the growth cycle. Road haulage of timber to mills now accounts for 67 per cent of timber transport, railways for 32 per cent, with timber floating only 1 per cent.

Norway's 66,600 km^2 of forest is less than 30 per cent of the Swedish total, but is still extensive in comparison with most European countries. Over 80 per cent is coniferous with growth rates declining northwards, as in Sweden. Most production is in the eastern interior, especially Hedmark and Oppland counties, and in Trøndelag. Of Norway's forest area, 84 per cent is privately owned, including 23 per cent in small forests under 50 hectares, mainly in combined forest and farm units. Most of the 10 per cent State-owned forest is in the north. Total annual production in 1988 (at 11.1 million m^3) was about 15 per cent higher than in previous years.

Over half of Denmark's small forested area of 4,930 km^2 is coniferous, mainly spruce. Of the forest area, 58 per cent is privately owned, one third in small forests under 50 hectares, whilst 30 per cent is State owned. Annual production in 1988 was a typical 1.9 million m^3.

2.2 Fisheries

The major renewable natural resource of Norway and western Denmark is the huge stock of fish that thrives on the relatively shallow and plankton-rich offshore waters of the North Sea and North Atlantic coasts. Ninety per cent of Norway's population lives on or near the coast, with the original settlement mainly based on a dual economy of fishing and subsistence agriculture.

Norway has traditionally dominated Scandinavian fishing, and accounted for two thirds of the catch until 1970 (Table 2.3). Norway's fish catch doubled in the 1960s from its (then) post-war average of 1.5 million tonnes per year to 3 million tonnes per year. This was due to the development of larger-decked vessels, nylon nets and lines, echo sounders to detect fish shoals and the greater use of deep-sea waters. Territorial waters under national control had also increased from 3 to 12 miles (about 5 to 19 km) in 1958. Most of the increased catch was of non-

Table 2.3 Sea fishing, 1960−88 (thousand tonnes landed)

	1960	1970	1980	1988
Denmark	574	1,220	1,983	1,963
Norway	1,486	2,910	2,400	1,735
Sweden	259	284	231	240

Source: *Yearbook of Nordic Statistics* (1989−90).

edible fish, such as capelin, which counted for two thirds of Norway's fish catch in 1970, and this is used to produce fish-meal fertilizers, fish oil or animal feed. Increased productivity resulted in fishing employment halving from 85,000 in 1948, of which 17,000 were part time, to 43,000 in 1970, of which 11,000 were part time.

After 1970 the total catch fell to only 2.4 million tonnes in 1980, in spite of the extension of territorial waters from 12 to 200 miles (about 19 to 320 km) in 1977. A further decline to 1.7 million tonnes in 1988 was mainly due to overfishing and mostly affected non-edible fish catches, which declined to about half the total. However, the important Lofoten cod fisheries had already collapsed from 51,000 tonnes in 1983 to only 15,000 tonnes in 1986, although the national catch of cod still represented one third of Norway's 5 billion Nkr fish sales in 1988. Half of Norway's edible fish catch is frozen, with frozen fish exported mainly to the USA and Britain, and fresh fish to France. Traditional salted, smoked and dried cod are still exported to catholic countries in southern Europe. In 1990 Norway's lowest-ever cod quotas were announced and haddock fishing was banned for the season off the Finnmark coast.

Half of Norway's fishing catch, value and employment are in north Norway, with half of this catch in lower-value capelin from the Barents Sea. West Norway is the second most important fishing area, with nearly one third of the fish catch and value, mainly in Møre and Romsdal county. Many settlements along parts of the Norwegian coast, mainly in the north and especially in Finnmark county, depend entirely on fishing, fish processing and distribution. The use of large trawlers is restricted to protect the livelihood of these small fishing settlements. As a result, small fishing vessels still predominate in Norway, with 88 per cent of the 9,000 decked vessels under 25 gross tonnes and only 6 per cent above 100 gross tonnes. Although fishing employment has declined further to 29,300 in 1988 (of which 7,300 are part time), productivity is only half the Danish level. EC membership would open up Norway's territorial waters between 12 miles and 200 miles (about 19 and 320 km) to EC trawlers and factory ships under the Common Fisheries Policy, and could wipe out the economic basis of many local settlements unless strict regionally based fishing plans were agreed. The 'no' vote in the 1972 EC referendum not surprisingly exceeded 80 per cent in most fishing settlements. Direct support to the fishing industry by the Norwegian government totalled 1,251 million NKr in 1985.

The huge success of salmon and rainbow-trout fish farming, especially in west Norway, has partly compensated for the 20-year decline in conventional fishing. Since the fish farmers formed a joint sales organization in 1978, exports of salmon grew to 100,000 tonnes in 1988, with 150,000 tonnes predicted for 1990.

The international ban on whaling after 1987 and the international controversies over both seal culling and the fur trade, have all reduced further employment and income in many fishing districts. In 1990 Norway unsuccessfully applied to catch up to 2,000 minke whales a year to help fish stocks recover.

Danish fishing more than tripled its output from 0.6 million tonnes in 1960 to almost 2 million tonnes per year from 1980. In 1988 Denmark exceeded Norway's output for the first time. Nearly half of Denmark's edible fish catch is cod. However, 80 per cent of the total catch is low-value, non-edible fish and so the 4 billion DKr value in 1988 was 20 per cent less than Norway's. This still represents 0.6 per cent of Denmark's gross national product (GNP) – one tenth of agriculture's contribution. All of Denmark's coastal waters are fished, with 73 per cent of the catch from the North Sea and 14 per cent from the Skaggerak. EC membership has given Danish fishermen access to many additional fish stocks, especially in the North Sea. The 15,300 fishermen in 1975 (of which 3,900 were part time) are equivalent to only half of the Norwegian total. Denmark's 3,000 fishing boats are larger, with 10 per cent over 100 gross tonnes and 67 per cent between 5 and 25 gross tonnes. The main fishing ports by value order are Esbjerg, Hirtshals, Thyborøn, Skagen, Hanstholm new town and Hvide Sande, all on the west coast or north tip of Jutland, nearest the richest fishing grounds and where commercial farming opportunities are weakest because of poor soils.

Sweden's fish catch was a mere 240,000 tonnes in 1988, largely unchanged for thirty years and worth 746 million SKr, with cod and herring most important. Fishing off Sweden's short west coast has declined, with lower quotas to about half the catch by weight and value. In the Baltic, south-coast fisheries are more important than the less saline waters of the east coast. Baltic fisheries revived with the adoption of midline territorial waters in 1977, which increased both Sweden's fishing waters and catch. Fishing employed 4,300 in 1985, of which 700 were part time. Sweden's nearly 2,000 fishing boats are small, with 78 per cent under 25 gross tonnes, and only 5 per cent over 100 gross tonnes. Simrishamn and Karlskrona on the south Baltic coast are now the main fishing ports.

2.3   The withdrawal of incentives to settle marginal areas

The years between 1955 and 1970 marked a watershed in Scandinavia's rural development as long-established government incentives to create new rural settlement were stopped and reversed as each government adopted new incentives to abandon marginal rural settlement. This reflected a belated recognition of the change in Scandinavia from traditional economies, dominated by a rural population engaged in farming, forestry or fishing at largely subsistence levels, to rich, modern economies dominated by an urban population employed in manufacturing industry or services and supported by a smaller, more commercial, primary sector.

Stone (1965) defines the terms settling, stability and abandoning as respectively a net increase, a balance and a net decrease in the number of rural dwellings in a local area. Settling occurred on unoccupied land or as an intensification of use of existing land due mainly to the pressure of population growth in each country caused by a high birth rate and a steadily lower death rate. Although emigration to North America, especially from Norway and Sweden, provided an alternative destination for surplus rural population from the nineteenth century onwards, Scandinavian governments were keen to promote internal colonization both for strategic reasons and to maximize the exploitation of the rural resource base.

Abandoning occurs because of the specialization and mechanization of farming, fishing and forestry, which reduces labour requirements but increases the minimum size of economic production units. The development of hydro-electric dams submerges the valley pastures that are critical to animal rearing and therefore results in a disproportionate number of lost farms. Younger people, especially young adult women, migrate from marginal farms or marginal fishing settlements, for education, jobs, better living standards and a less physically demanding life. Population decline therefore usually occurs in marginal areas well before the abandonment of settlement. Age-selective migration leads to an ageing rural population and often to delayed abandoning, leasing or amalgamation of marginal farms when parents retire or die. The switch in government support away from settling to abandoning further encourages this rationalization process.

Denmark encouraged internal colonization with new settling in west Jutland after it lost Slesvig-Holstein, with its rich agricultural land, to Prussia in 1864. The Danish Heath Society encouraged the creation of new farms in the sandy heathland and, in 1868, the government created the new town and port of Esbjerg to export agricultural products to Britain. Marshes and peat bogs were also drained for agricultural use until the 1960s. Between 1900 and 1960, government financial support encouraged new settling throughout Denmark by creating an average 500 farms per year. This was largely through subdivision of existing farms and was the continuation of a process started by the Enclosure Act 1781. Until 1960, Danish legislation attempted with decreasing success to prevent farm amalgamation. Market forces were already promoting amalgamation to achieve economic-sized family farms, and small farms under ten hectares were declining rapidly. Until 1967, land leasing, to create viable-sized farms, was used less in Denmark than in Norway and

Sweden as the maximum permitted eight-year lease discouraged investment. Since then farmers can buy or lease land up to 75 hectares and can
lease further land within 15 km up to an overall total of 200 hectares.
The growth of city farmers, whose main income is non-agricultural,
has been stopped to protect the family freehold farm structure. Since
1960 the number of farms has halved to 84,000 in 1988 and the total
number of non-family farm workers had declined to less than 20,000.
Net migration from rural to urban areas ceased by 1970 as the supply of
surplus rural labour dried up.

Norway encouraged internal colonization by farmers and fishermen in
its uplands and also (after the 1751 northern Scandinavian international
boundary agreement) in its Arctic north and Lapland. Enclosure Acts in
1821 and 1857 and subdivision also created many new farms. During the
mid-nineteenth century, a temporarily harsher climate led to the
abandoning of some uneconomic farms at the margin of settlement.
From the 1850s on, population pressure from a high birth rate and
falling death rate, the abandoning of some marginal farms and land
consolidation all fuelled the flood of migrants to North America, although
settling continued. After 1920, the strategic threat in the north from
Communist USSR and the imposition of immigrant quotas by the USA
both stimulated new settling. Some 18,500 new farms were created
through Bureising, the State homesteading programmme, between 1920
and 1970, whilst the semi-private *Ny Jord* programme created 69 settlements and 601 farms between 1912 and 1969 to limit emigration
by promoting domestic colonization (Stone, 1971). New spot-settling
therefore continued with government support until 1970, long after the
peak period in the 1920s and 1930s. After temporary evacuation in
1945–6 of population from war-razed Finnmark and east Troms, all
settlements were recreated *in situ*. From the 1950s market forces encouraged the abandoning or amalgamation of farms and this was encouraged from 1961 by the Regional Development Fund's stimulation of
a more specialized and commercial rural economy. Since 1970, overfishing
and small fish quotas have hastened the decline of many coastal, rural
areas. However, Norway still retains a heavily subsidized and over-large
primary workforce and rural population. With the increasing likelihood
of Norwegian membership of the EC in the 1990s, and a diminishing
strategic threat from a reformed and less hostile Soviet Union, the
abandoning of many Norwegian farms and some small isolated fishing
villages should be anticipated.

Settlement was encouraged by the Swedish government for geopolitical
reasons from the late sixteenth century along the coast of northern
Sweden and to its then territory, Finland. From the mid-seventeenth
century, settlement extended via the river valleys inland in northern

Sweden, with two restrictions. The 1751 Lappmarksgränsen, or Sami Region boundary, created a national reserve of land to the north and west that roughly coincides with Stone's (1962) Inner and Middle Fringe Zone boundary in Norrbotten and Västerbotten counties. The 1867 Odlingsgränsen, or cultivation boundary, restricted new settling to the north west to reduce conflicts between Sami reindeer herders and farmers, and largely coincides with both Stone's (*ibid.*) Middle and Outer Fringe Zone boundary and the 800-day degrees of growth isoline (Figure 2.1). New farms were created by both enclosure and subdivision. Consolidation of fragmented holdings began with the Storskifte Acts of 1749 and 1757. Full enclosure began in Skåne and south of Lake Väner under the Enskifte Act 1803 and extended elsewhere under the Lagaskifte Act 1827.

After 1860, population pressure led to heavy emigration to North America, especially from south Sweden, but settling continued and peatlands were drained for cultivation between 1850 and 1950. To discourage emigration to the USA, planned colonies of new settlers were established after the First World War and, from 1916, subsidies were given to retain existing settlers west of the 1867 cultivation boundary to provide forestry workers, forest-fire protection and military intelligence. These subsidies were improved as late as 1948. New, small-farm settlements were also subsidized on State-owned forest land. A new inland railway was constructed through north Sweden in the 1930s, both to reduce isolation and for strategic defence. The earlier northern mainline railway, which had itself been built slightly inland from the coast as protection from invasion across the frozen Gulf to Bothnia from the then Russian-controlled Finland, was now thought to be vulnerable. Population had already reached its peak in south Norrland by 1920 and north Norrland by 1940 with heavy outmigration, especially to Stockholm. Free market abandoning had commenced in the 1930s and accelerated after the war years with arable land giving way to pasture or forest. An ambitious hydro-electric power (HEP) programme in the 1950s required many northern valleys for dams.

In 1955 Sweden withdrew incentives for small-farm settling and the Land Acquisition Act instead encouraged farm rationalization by county boards. Sales of farms were restricted to close family members, and to people with agricultural-college qualifications and a target farm size was set of 10−20 hectares of arable land. Some settlers on State land were paid to leave, and forest workers were brought in when required. After 1955 there was a strong rural population decline and widespread abandoning occurred inland, and isolated abandoning occurred between coastal towns where many farms became summer cottages. The extent of rural population decline is masked by the creation of huge municipalities with health and education services provided in the growing municipal town for remote rural areas. Norling (1960) attributed abandoning in inland Västerbotten between 1930 and 1959 30 per cent to age, illness or death, 20 per cent to low income, 20 per cent to poor roads, 15 per cent to poor houses and 8 per cent to HEP developments.

In 1959 farm target size was increased to between 25 and 40 hectares. Acreage subsidies replaced milk subsidies in 1960 and covered up to 60 per cent of farm costs in northern Sweden, but from 1963 were focused on the more economic farms. The only new settlement allowed was for mining, hydro-electric stations or military purposes. A stronger Land Acquisition Act was passed in 1965. A Land Management Act also gave State credit guarantees and, in northern Sweden, sometimes also grants. This rural support was given to agriculture, forestry, horticulture, fishing and reindeer herding to generate employment for a permanent population.

Since 1950 the number of Swedish farm holdings has declined by nearly two thirds to 101,000 in 1988 and over half the arable land has been lost from the interior of northern Sweden. More marginal land has been made uneconomic by a near doubling of crop yields per hectare from 1950 to 1975 due to more productive crop strains, fertilizers, pesticides and land drainage.

Although after 35 years Swedish agricultural rationalization and settlement restructuring is more advanced than in Norway, net outmigration to the south is still continuing, albeit at lower levels. Although north Swedish population totals are now relatively stable, this masks continuing growth of large coastal towns, such as Umeå, and selective decline elsewhere. If Sweden joins the EC, the CAP would accelerate farm abandoning, especially in the north. Sweden's historic and expensive policy of armed neutrality has also concentrated defence spending and boosted settlement in the north; although Sweden is likely to remain neutral, its defence expenditure may decline as the strategic threat from the Soviet Union recedes, thereby reducing another support to north-Swedish settlement.

2.4   Pollution, acid rain and the environment

Dying trees, dead lakes, photochemical smog, offshore algae blooms that kill fish and marine life, and the contamination of vegetation and animals by nuclear fallout, are some of the consequences of the pollution of the Scandinavian environment that have emerged in the last twenty years. Scandinavians are aware of and concerned about global and regional threats to the environment and all three governments have taken a lead in pollution-control measures and global initiatives. The then Norwegian

Prime Minister, Gro Harlem Brundtland, chaired the World Commission on Environment and Development, which produced its report, *Our Common Future*, in April 1987.

Acid rain results from the emission of sulphur dioxide and nitrogen oxides from the burning of oil, coal and gas by power stations, transport and industry (Muniz, Seip and Samstag, 1989). Acid levels in Europe in 1985 were twice those of 1955. In Scandinavia, most harm has occurred in Norway and in southern Sweden where thin soils have insufficient lime to neutralize the acid rain, which leaches out nutrients, releases poisonous metals and drains off into rivers and lakes. Acid rain first damaged fish stocks in lakes; now all lakes and rivers in a 18,000-km^2 area of southernmost Norway have lost nearly all their fish, whilst rivers and lakes in eastern Finnmark are being damaged by Soviet pollution. One fifth of Sweden's 90,000 lakes are at risk. Forest damage, which includes reduced crown density as well as areas of dead trees, is a serious threat to forestry − which is Sweden's main natural resource and an important natural resource in Norway. By 1988 only half of Norway's trees had full-density crowns and, in some counties, well under 40 per cent. Acid water also corrodes drinking-water pipes, whilst air pollution in urban areas damages health, buildings and cars. Although Sweden has tackled some of the symptoms of acid rain by liming lakes at great expense, the problems needs to be tackled at source. Seventy per cent of Sweden's sulphur-dioxide pollution comes from foreign power stations, whilst 90 per cent of Norway's acid rain is caused by emissions in other countries, principally power stations and factories in Great Britain, Germany and Eastern Europe. However, local vehicle exhausts are the principal source of nitrogen oxide.

In pollution control, Scandinavia is well ahead of the international community. For example, Norway will have reduced its 1980 sulphur-dioxide emissions by 50 per cent by 1993 compared with a European and North American target of at least 30 per cent. Norway's nitrogen-oxide emissions will be cut by 30 per cent between 1986 and 1998. From 1989 all petrol-driven cars in Norway and Sweden have to be fitted with catalytic convertors, whilst lead-free petrol has been the norm since 1986. Stricter controls on diesel emissions from buses and lorries are planned for 1992 and 1994. Neighbouring countries, such as Britain, are slowly responding to Scandinavian pressure to control and filter power-station and factory emissions that fall on Scandinavia.

An increase in greenhouse gases threatens to bring global warming, a changing climate and rising sea levels. Scandinavia banned the use of CFCs as aerosol propellants in the early 1980s and their CFC emissions will virtually cease by 1995. Carbon-dioxide emissions, from the burning of fossil fuels, are harder to control. Denmark has taken a lead by converting thermal power stations from coal or oil to natural-gas firing, and by developing renewable energy in the form of wind power and waste burning. The widespread but controlled incineration of domestic refuse in Denmark in district-heating plants is less hazardous than the combination of landfill dumps that produce future methane problems and the use of fossil fuels for heating. In Norway, however, the largest producers of carbon dioxide are the flaring-off of gas from the Ekofisk and Statfjord oil and gas fields, and the Mongstad oil refinery.

The fallout from the Chernobyl nuclear-reactor fire in 1986 resulted in widespread radioactive contamination of soil, vegetation and animals, especially in Norway and northern Sweden (Edin, 1987). As caesium has a half life of thirty years, radioactivity in 1990 remained two to three times the pre-Chernobyl level in Norwegian soil and in Norway and northern Sweden much reindeer, sheep and cattle meat remains unfit for human consumption. Norway is now concerned that the Soviet Union will move its nuclear testing ground from Kazakhstan back to its former Soviet Arctic site that, in the 1950s, was a source of radioactive contamination over Scandinavia. Accidental oil slicks from oil exploration and production and from merchant shipping are increasingly likely as oil exploration reaches into the southern Barents Sea with its long harsh winters and occasional icebergs. Over 50,000 seabirds died in the Skaggerak after the discharge of ballast water by the Greek tanker, *Stylis*, in 1980, whilst the shipwreck of the *Mercantile Marcia* off Sognefjord in autumn 1989 cost 30 million NKr to clear up and destroyed an unknown quantity of marine life. Controls on other marine pollution were agreed in 1987 for the heavily polluted North Sea by all countries. A 50-per-cent reduction of toxic chemical and nutrient discharge was agreed by 1995 and an end to the dumping of hazardous industrial waste and the incineration of industrial waste by 1994. Better sewage treatment and a reduction in the use of agricultural fertilizers lowered the over-enrichment of rivers and lakes with nitrogen in the 1980s. Ground-water pollution remains the hidden time bomb. Pesticides are now used more selectively and the use of DDT was banned in 1975. However, in the late 1980s the sudden growth of temporary algae blooms in the coastal waters of the Baltic, Skaggerak and Kattegat killed fish by depriving them of oxygen and destroyed bathing beaches. In 1989, for example, 450 to 500 tonnes of farmed salmon were killed off Rogaland in south-west Norway. Norwegian fish farming, mainly of salmon, has itself led to pollution problems from waste feed and faeces.

A larger investment is now being made to treat industrial effluent and domestic sewage. In Norway a $6-billion programme announced in 1990 includes $1.5 billion for sewage disposal, $1.2 billion for waste disposal, $460 million for industry and $460 million for agriculture. The cost of some industrial pollution controls is enormous and will bring lower profits, smaller market share and possible bankruptcy unless international competitors apply the same controls. Borregaard, with a mercury by-product, and Norsk Hydro, with a dioxide by-product, are two prominent Norwegian examples. Nevertheless, Sweden in 1988 ordered a 50-per-cent reduction in chlorine pollutants, a product of bleaching in the pulp and paper industry.

Recycling waste is increasingly important. Norway, for example, recycles 25 per cent of its waste paper, 4 per cent of plastics and 7 per cent of glass, including most glass bottles, which all carry a compulsory deposit. To deter the dumping of old cars, a returnable deposit on cars is repaid in Norway when disposed of at a breaker's yard whilst, since 1975, Swedish vehicle owners have received a 500-SKr premium when vehicles are scrapped (Swedish Institute, 1988d).

Scandinavian concern about the environment has resulted in numerous government policy changes, single-issue campaigns and the emergence through proportional representation of the Green Party in the Swedish parliament in 1988, with 5.5 per cent of the vote and twenty MPs. Since 1985, Greens have also gained a small but growing foothold in Swedish and Danish local government, especially in the main urban areas.

2.5 The Lapp (Sami) economy and way of life

The Lapps, or Sami, of northern Scandinavia are a nomadic people with a distinctive language from the same Finno-Ugric group as Finnish, Estonian and Hungarian. They migrated to Scandinavia from the east about 3,000 years ago with an economy based on hunting, especially reindeer, and fishing. Reindeer herding and breeding developed with some semi-domestication of wild reindeer and the adoption of a semi-nomadic life-style. This is probably the most effective, ecologically sound use of Scandinavia's mountain and forest fringe area.

The number of Sami is now about 50,000, including 25,000–30,000 in Norway, 15,000–17,000 in Sweden, about 4,000 in Finland and a further 2,000 in the Soviet Union. However, the area of settlement is extensive, with Sami scattered in small groups throughout the whole of Arctic Scandinavia and Arctic Finland, and inland southwards down both sides of the Scandinavian mountain spine to 62°N at Idre in Dalarna in Sweden and at neighbouring Femunden in Hedmark in Norway. After the international boundaries were agreed in northern Scandinavia in 1751, Sami were given the right to cross them seasonally with their herds. This right was withdrawn between Finland and Norway in 1852 but is still retained between Norway and Sweden.

The Sami are now mainly sedentary and can be divided into three groups, namely Mountain Sami and Forest Sami who are reindeer breeders, and Fisher Sami who fish the coastal waters of parts of north Norway and inland rivers and lakes, and who also farm. The Mountain Sami are the true reindeer herders but nomads now only total about 2,800 in Norway, 2,500 in Sweden and a few hundred in Finland. They follow the reindeer long distances along the main north west-south east aligned river and lake systems to summer pastures in the high mountains, or on the Norwegian coast from and back to spring and autumn grazing lands in the thin birch forests and low mountains and to winter pastures in the coniferous forests (Figure 2.1).

The Sami village is both an administrative and economic unit and a grazing area (Swedish Institute, 1988e). It is responsible co-operatively for reindeer breeding and common facilities. Most Sami settlement is in the thin birch-forest belt where reindeer mating, calving and slaughtering occur. Forest Sami settlement, however, occurs in some of the winter pasture areas within the coniferous forest, especially in parts of Norrbotten, in locations more accessible to the rest of Scandinavia. In Sweden in 1986, 77 per cent of the 286,000 reindeer were owned by Mountain Sami, 16 per cent by Forest Sami and the remainder by Sami living in concession villages. Many Sami now work in other occupations. A Nordic Sami Council was founded in Karasjok in 1956 and meets every three years, whilst a Nordic Co-operation Agency was established in 1965 and, in 1974, a joint Nordic Sami Institute for Research was set up at Kautokeino, also in northern Norway (Nesheim, 1981). Sami are also represented on the World Council of Indigenous People (the 'Fourth World') established in 1975. Education is provided for Sami children in fixed and nomadic State-run schools, and the Sami language is promoted. Under a Sami language law, Norwegian Samis gained the legal right in February 1991 to be taught in their own language and to use it in all dealings with official bodies (Smith, 1991). Norwegian Samis already had their own television and radio stations and several daily and weekly Sami newspapers are published in the Nordic countries.

Since the 1960s, the use of snowmobiles, radio transmitters, light planes and helicopters has speeded up reindeer herding. The number of reindeer in the winter herd grew between 1980 and 1986 from 214,000 to 286,000 in Sweden, and from 170,000 to 243,000 in Norway. Despite the premium price paid for reindeer meat by urban Scandinavians, a herd of 500 reindeer is needed to support a Sami family at an average income level, but the average herd is less than 300. Radioactive fallout from the Chernobyl nuclear accident in 1986 onto Arctic vegetation led to a ban on reindeer meat and fish sales for human consumption whilst caesium contamination continued. Government compensation will be needed for many years to sustain the Sami way of life.

There has also been growing conflict between reindeer herding and the development of hydro-electric dams (which flood winter pasture), tourism, new roads and road traffic, intensive forestry and the protection of predatory animals. In Sweden the 1971 reindeer-husbandry law tries to safeguard Sami interests, and there is now a ban on new hydro-electric dams in Sweden. In Norway the conflict over the Alta River HEP dam in the late 1970s led to a decade of pressure for greater rights for Sami people and more self-assertion. Sami rights were enhanced by two Norwegian Supreme Court decisions in favour of compensation for lost reindeer grazing areas and the right to hunt and fish. In both Norway and Sweden, however, the Sami's right of ownership of traditional Sami land is vigorously disputed. In September 1989 the first election took place to the 39 member Sameting – Norway's Sami People's Congress. Although more authoritative than its non-elected predecessor, the Norwegian Sami Council, the Sameting, is still only advisory. However, in protest at a special census, only 5,500 Sami, out of 25,000–30,000, registered to vote at the first election.

THREE

The Transition to a Post-Industrial Economy

3.1 Energy

Scandinavia now produces more energy than it consumes for the first time since industrialization began on a small scale in the mid-nineteenth century, using coal imported at great expense from Britain. Scandinavia's turnround in the 1980s from net energy importer to net energy exporter is due to Norway's emergence as a major oil and natural-gas producer and exporter (Figure 3.1). The distributions of energy resources, supply and consumption are different in Denmark, Norway and Sweden and continue to change rapidly.

Historically, Scandinavia's energy resources were poor as it lacked coal deposits and so nineteenth-century industrialization was slow. The only indigenous supplies of energy were then charcoal, wood, peat and direct water power. Charcoal's use was controlled by each government because of its vital role in the absence of coal, especially as a reducing agent in the iron-making industry. By the late 1800s Sweden alone was using 5 million m^3 of timber a year in charcoal production, mainly for the Bergslagen iron industries.

Around 1880, new technology allowed water power to be converted into electricity for use on site. This hydro-electric power (HEP) provided the energy base for Scandinavia's industrialization and, by 1910, there were numerous small HEP stations on rivers throughout Norway and Sweden. HEP potential, however, varies enormously from very high in southern Norway and northern Sweden to virtually non-existent in Denmark. Norway fares better overall than Sweden because of less winter freezing, higher precipitation, a higher head of water and less evaporation. As electricity could not be transmitted long distances until the 1950s, the metal-smelting, electro-chemical and wood-processing industries were forced to locate at or near hydro-electric sites, which were often in remote areas. Thermal power stations, using imported coal, were built in areas without HEP and, from 1912, an Øresund cable linked east Denmark and Sweden. This gave Copenhagen access to cheap

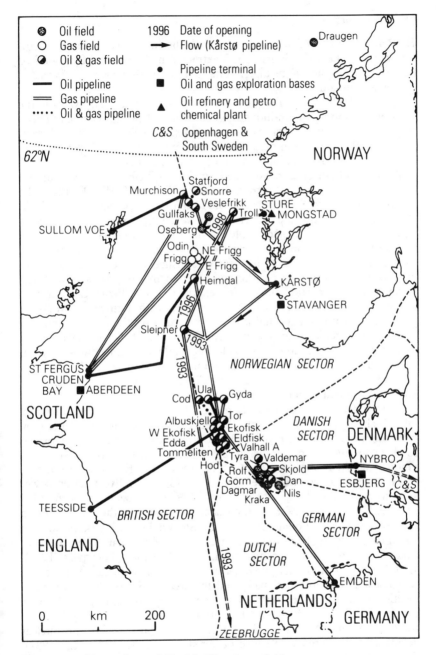

Figure 3.1 Norwegian and Danish oil and gas fields

HEP and south Sweden access to Danish thermal power at times of low water. Since the 1920s Norway has extracted high-cost coal from limited reserves on Svalbard in the high Arctic, but production has never exceeded domestic demand.

From 1950 to 1973 the demand for energy rose sharply with the rapidly developing urban-industrial economies of Scandinavia and cheap imported oil replaced coal as the major fossil fuel. In the period from 1965 to 1973, for example, energy demand rose by 49 per cent in Norway from 13.2 million tonnes of coal equivalent (MTCE) to 19.7 MTCE, by 44 per cent in Sweden from 34.5 MTCE to 49.7 MTCE and by 43 per cent in Denmark from 19.5 MTCE to 27.9 MTCE. From the 1950s, Norway and Sweden accelerated their development of larger HEP stations, whilst national electricity grids were built covering the whole of Sweden, including undersea cables to the islands of Gotland and Öland, the southern two thirds of Norway and separately for east and west Denmark (Figure 3.2). Nordel was established in 1963 as an advisory organization to promote Nordic co-operation in the production, distribution and consumption of electrical energy (Taylor, 1974). Co-operation reduces the total reserve capacity required with immense savings in power-station investment and a reduced burden on the environment. In total, 22 international grid links have been built in Scandinavia with a total capacity over 5,500 MW, including undersea connections between Jutland and both Gothenburg and southern Norway and land links from Jutland to Germany and Sweden to Finland. However, west and east Denmark remain unconnected.

Sweden decided in the 1960s to reduce its overdependence on imported oil, which supplied 70 per cent of its energy in 1970, making it more oil dependent than any other major industrial country. Sweden chose instead to develop nuclear power using Swedish uranium. This decision was vindicated when the Organization of Petroleum Exporting Countries (OPEC) quadrupled the price of oil in 1973–4. Twelve nuclear power stations with a total capacity of 9,500 MW were opened between 1972 and 1985 on four market-oriented sites. Ringhals south of Gothenburg has four reactors, Forsmark north of Stockholm and Oskarshamn in south-east Sweden have three reactors each, whilst Barsebäck north of Malmö, and opposite Copenhagen, has two reactors (Törnqvist, 1986). In the mid-1970s the emerging environmental groups organized opposition to nuclear power internationally and in Sweden. Sweden's 1976 general election resulted in the anti-nuclear Centre Party forming part of a new centre and right government. The growing anti-nuclear lobby forced a referendum in 1980 on the future of nuclear power after the nuclear accident at the Three Mile Island power station in the USA (Edin, 1987). This referendum resolved that no further nuclear power stations would

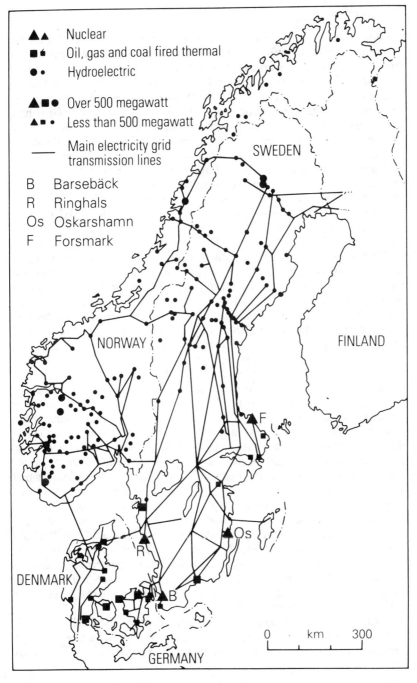

Figure 3.2 Electricity production and transmission

be built, and that the twelve existing reactors would be phased out between 1995 and 2010. The 1986 Chernobyl nuclear accident further strengthened Sweden's anti-nuclear lobby.

Meanwhile HEP was becoming increasingly expensive as most of the untapped potential was in the far north and required huge dams, while the main markets were in the more heavily populated south. Grid links were expensive to build and over 10 per cent of power was lost in transmission. During the 1970s the drowning of more farmland and pastures for HEP dams provoked such vociferous opposition from conservation groups and Sami (Lapps) that the Swedish government agreed to limit severely further HEP development. The main reserve capacity of 3,813 MW is on the Torne, Kalix, Pite and Vinde Rivers, but only 8 MW had been developed by 1986. During the 1980s, HEP output was static, whilst nuclear power nearly tripled as the final reactors came on stream (Table 3.1). This left the Swedish government in a quandary as HEP accounts for half of Swedish electricity supply, while most of the rest is nuclear generated. The emphasis now is on developing indigenous biomass fuels such as timber waste, peat and domestic refuse and on district water-heating systems to replace electric heating systems. In the mid-1980s, 13 per cent of Swedish electricity was generated by burning wood, peat and the residue from paper mills (Törnqvist, 1986). Wind and solar energy is also being developed and, since 1985, natural gas has been imported by pipeline into southern Sweden from Denmark. Energy-saving schemes include triple glazing and 20-cm-thick wall and roof insulation in homes and offices. Sweden appears to be on the verge of a self-inflicted energy crisis that will require a partial return to increased oil imports, the development of natural-gas imports from Norway and more energy-saving schemes. In late 1990 the Social Democratic government, in a major policy change, decided to postpone the first nuclear-power shutdowns planned for the mid-1990s. This was to protect Sweden's energy-intensive export industries, such as pulp and paper making, which otherwise faced a doubling of electricity prices, a loss of competitiveness and close down (*The Economist*, 1990).

After the 1973 energy crisis, total Swedish energy demand fell nearly 10 per cent from 1,385,000 terrajoules (TJ) to 1,250,000 TJ in 1982 and 1983, but rose again to 1,383,000 TJ in 1987. In 1988 Sweden produced about 60 per cent of its primary energy needs. Oil imports accounted for four fifths of the energy deficit (Table 3.1). Oil products still accounted for 40 per cent of energy consumption and electrical energy 31 per cent, half of which was HEP.

In the 1960s Norway already had western Europe's best HEP potential with most of it still to develop, and HEP was Norway's biggest single resource. From 1969 onwards, Norway's energy resources were trans-

Table 3.1 Production of primary energy, 1980 and 1988 (000s TJ)

	Solid fuels	Crude oil	Gases	District heating	Nuclear power	HEP	Total primary energy production	Gross inland supply
Denmark 1980	3	13	0	0	0	0	16	762
1988	37	202	97	0	0	0	336	774
Norway 1980	23	1,084	1,079	0	0	355	2,541	803
1988	45	2,400	1,191	0	0	394	4,030	883
Sweden 1980	135	0	0	0	275	248	658	1,763
1988	233	0	0	24*	719	251	1,227	2,046

* Input to heat pump.
Source: *Yearbook of Nordic Statistics* (1981 and 1989–90).

by the discovery of large reserves of offshore oil and natural gas North Sea up to 62° N, which replaced HEP as Norway's largest ce. Exploration north of 62° N was deferred for a variety of reasons including much rougher weather and deeper water in the North Atlantic than in the North Sea, and concern about oil spillages in the rich northern fishing grounds (EFTA, 1979). Norway's oil production from Ekofisk field began in 1971 and, after 1975, production exceeded Norway's domestic oil consumption (Figure 3.1). Parliament agreed in 1974 to set a moderate production limit of 90 million tonnes of oil equivalent (TOE) to conserve reserves and to a cautious use of oil revenues in domestic consumption in a largely unsuccessful attempt to limit demand inflation and to protect Norwegian industry from an over-strong, oil-rich currency. Parliament also agreed to a State majority in future exploration and production and to an increased State role in oil refining and petrochemical plants (Stenstadvold, 1977).

Pipeline technology had not progressed enough to cross the 700-m-deep submarine trench between the oilfields and the Norwegian coast. Instead, Ekofisk oil was piped to Teesside in England from 1975 and then part shipped back to Norwegian refineries. Ekofisk natural gas was piped to Emden in West Germany from 1977 as the West Germans offered a better price than Britain and there was no Norwegian market for gas. Frigg natural gas was piped to St Fergus in Scotland from 1977, whilst oil from the giant Statfjord field was shipped out by tanker from 1979. In the 1980s pipeline technology advanced to enable the submarine Norwegian trench to be crossed. In 1986 a separation unit was opened at Kårstø south of Haugesund to convert rich gas, piped from the Gullfaks field, into dry gas to be piped to the Heimdal–Ekofisk–Emden pipeline. In 1989 the first oil pipeline to Norway was opened between the Oseberg field and Sture, north of Bergen, to feed the nearby Mongstad oil refinery. Mongstad's rural island location is controversial as it is beyond the commuting range of Bergen, and the refinery cost $1.7 billion, $1 billion above the estimate. Other pipelines opened include gas from the mainly British, but partly Norwegian, Murchison field to St Fergus in Scotland, and oil from Murchison to Sullom Voe in the Shetland Islands, and Heimdal to Cruden Bay in Scotland. A new gas pipeline is being built from Troll and Sleipner to Zeebrugge in Belgium. Future gas developments should include a recommended undersea pipeline from Kårstø to Gothenburg to serve the Swedish market, and a new pipeline to either Eemshaven in The Netherlands or Emden to deliver already-contracted gas to western Europe by the late 1990s.

Norwegian oil and gas production climbed from 10 million TOE in 1975 to 50 million TOE in 1980, almost equally gas and oil, of which three quarters was from the Ekofisk area. As Ekofisk declined after 1980, production shifted northwards, Statfjord becoming the largest oil producer in 1983 and Frigg the largest gas producer in 1984 (Knowles, 1985). By 1988 production reached 83 million TOE, including 55.5 million tonnes of oil, over half from the Statfjord field. New exploration north and south of 62° N started in 1980 to prolong the anticipated oil-production peak beyond 1990. By November 1989, 4.5 billion TOE had been discovered in the Norwegian sector south of 62° N, of which 3 billion TOE were commercial, including 760 million TOE that had already been produced (Royal Ministry of Petroleum and Energy (RMPE), 1990). A further 0.9 billion TOE are expected to be discovered. North of 62° N, 480 million TOE, 46 per cent of it oil, had been discovered off mid-Norway in the Haltenbanken area at 64−5° N and a further 1.5 billion TOE are anticipated. However, the cost of production and transport has delayed their development. Only the Draugen oilfield has so far been approved for development with oil delivery by tankers loading offshore. In the Arctic in the Tromsøflaket area at 71−2° N, 270 million TOE, 97 per cent of it gas, had been discovered by 1989 but none is yet commercial. A further 1.6 billion TOE are anticipated in the Arctic and, in 1990, oil was discovered further north in the Lopparyggen area of the Barents Sea. Most oil and gas production therefore will remain south of 62° N, because of long delivery distances and high transport costs, until long-term oil and gas prices recover from their mid-1980s slump. Iraq's invasion of Kuwait in August 1990 temporarily more than doubled crude oil prices to $37 per barrel. However, after the subsequent and brief 1991 Gulf War, prices fell back to previous levels.

In 1990 Norway had half of Europe's proven gas reserves and 60 per cent of its oil reserves. Although Norway's record oil production of 1.7 million barrels per day in 1990 should rise further to 1.95 million in 1991 and can be sustained until 1994, it will then drop without new discoveries to only 650,000 barrels per day by the year 2000. Natural-gas production, in contrast, will double to 60 million m³ by 2005 and Norway is already the world's third largest natural-gas exporter after the Soviet Union and Canada.

Norway's centre and right government expanded exploration and production in 1990 by tendering the largest number of new blocks since 1965, by advancing the development of the Brage oilfield from 1990 to 1993 and by developing the Statfjord East and North oilfields. The Veslefrikk and Troll West fields also started production.

Oil and gas have transformed the Norwegian economy, contributing 2.5 per cent of gross domestic product (GDP) in 1975, rising to a peak of 19 per cent in 1984 but dropping back to 10.1 per cent by 1987 following the halving of oil prices in 1986. Fluctuating oil prices caused economic instability: oil and gas accounted for half of Norway's exports in 1984 and 1985, dropping back to 40 per cent in 1986 and 37 per cent in 1987. Petroleum royalties and taxes yielded 35 billion NKr in 1985, but only 10 billion NKr the following year. In the early 1980s, oil wealth enabled Norwegians, for the first time, to surpass temporarily the Swedes as Scandinavia's richest people, with Scandinavia's strongest currency. Unemployment remained below 3 per cent, service-sector jobs increased by 40 per cent over ten years whilst oil revenues provided huge subsidies for regional development, agriculture, fisheries and manufacturing industries. Oil and gas wealth also brought problems. High wage rates and a strong oil currency priced Norwegian manufactured exports out of world markets while the oil industry outbid other industries for key workers. Oil-related jobs in exploration, production, servicing, rig-building and refining totalled 58,000 in 1989, compared with a peak of 65,000 in 1987, still representing over 2 per cent of the national workforce, with nearly half in Rogaland county including the main oil centre of Stavanger (RMPE, 1990; Figure 3.1). Most oil workers are Norwegians employed by Statoil (100 per cent State owned), Norsk Hydro (51 per cent State owned) and the private Norwegian company, Saga Petroleum (Helle, 1989). The small number of processing jobs reflects the limited size of the Norwegian market for refined oil and petrochemical products. After the oil-price slump in 1986, government spending was reduced and unemployment soared to its 1990 record levels whilst the value of the Norwegian currency fell back below both the Swedish and Danish currency.

Norway's economy was insulated by its huge oil and gas wealth from the deflationary effects of the 1973 OPEC price rise. Unlike Denmark and Sweden, Norway's energy demand consequently continued to grow after 1973, rising 32 per cent from 534,000 TJ in 1973 to 706,000 TJ in 1987.

Although Norway's oil and gas boom has created an energy supply nearly five times Norway's requirements, HEP still dominates Norway's own energy consumption, with 48 per cent of the market in 1988 (Table 3.1). Industry uses half the electricity with electro-metallurgical and electrochemical industries accounting for two thirds of industrial consumption. Oil products account for 41 per cent of energy consumption, whilst gas consumption is just starting. Norway's impressive 25,000 MW of HEP capacity is mainly in large stations over 100 MW, including very large stations such as Sima with 1,120 MW. Although this capacity represents only about 60 per cent of Norway's HEP potential, new developments in the 1980s have been limited by environmental concerns, by conflict with Sami in the north, and by opposition from the tourist industry in the south and west, where the most economic sites remain.

The lack of both fossil fuels and HEP potential had delayed and limited the development of an industrial economy in Denmark. Nearly all of Denmark's energy supplies were imported, initially mainly coal, but from the 1950s mainly oil. By 1973 cheap imported oil constituted 87 per cent of Denmark's energy imports and fuels accounted for 14 per cent of all imports by value. OPEC's quadrupling of oil prices in 1973–4, therefore, hit Denmark even harder than Sweden, especially as Denmark had rejected nuclear power. Denmark's dearth of fossil fuels had ironically ended in 1972 with the discovery of limited reserves of oil and gas in the Danish sector of the North Sea, but significant production took another seven years for oil, and ten years for gas. In the meantime the Danish economy had gone into recession as the government tried various ways to reduce its dependency on imported oil. Power stations were converted back to coal firing, using cheap imported coal from Poland and South Africa, imports rising from 2.2 million tonnes in 1972 to 7.8 million tonnes in 1979. National campaigns to reduce temperatures in offices and homes to 19°C were successful and insulation standards were increased. District heating of apartments and private houses became widespread in all major urban areas using water heated by domestic-refuse incinerators and from power-station cooling systems. Biomass incinerators from 10 to 1,750 KW output have been developed to burn straw, straw pellets or wood chips, as well as pelleted urban refuse or coal to heat factories, homes and greenhouses (*Denmark Review*, 1988). Denmark's energy demand fell by 25 per cent from 690,000 TJ in 1973 to 520,000 TJ in 1983, rising again to 595,000 TJ in 1987 – still 14 per cent less than in 1973.

Danish oil production from its Gorm, Skold and Dan fields reached 2 million tonnes in 1983 rising to 4.8 million tonnes in 1988, whilst oil imports fell from 14 million tonnes in 1980 to 5.1 million tonnes (Figure 3.1). This compares with Denmark's oil-refinery capacity of 8.3 million tonnes. Gas production started from Denmark's Tyra and Roar fields in 1982 rising to 2.5 billion m³ by 1988. Oil and gas production are both piped to Nybro north of Esbjerg and an overland natural-gas pipeline was opened to Copenhagen and south Sweden in 1985. An internal market for gas was created by converting power stations to gas firing, which also reduced air pollution. Domestic and industrial use of gas had also started while, by 1988, 0.8 million m³ was exported per year to Sweden. By 1988 Denmark was, therefore, nearly half self-sufficient in oil, had a surplus of gas, and was 43 per cent self-sufficient in overall energy production (Table 3.1).

Seven more oilfields are being brought into production in the south-west Danish sector and three new gas and oilfields in the north sector with near self-sufficiency in oil achievable by 1992 and projected annual revenues to the government of 3 billion DKr. A third round of exploration licences were tendered in 1989, charges were lowered to keep Danish oil and gas competitive and royalties were abolished.

Alternative energy sources have also been vigorously promoted. Denmark has become a world centre for wind power with 100 MW of modern, aerodynamic three-sail windmills developed by 1990. A second phase of development is planned and a useful high-technology export industry has been created (*Denmark Review*, 1989). Geothermal heat is being used from a 1,250-m-deep borehole to serve a district-heating scheme at Thisted in north Jutland, in conjunction with an absorption heat pump. This 2-million-GJ resource should last twenty-five years and represents 0.0005 per cent of Denmark's usable geothermal reserves (*Denmark Review*, 1988).

In twenty-five years Denmark has transformed itself from a massive energy importer with an overwhelmingly oil-dominated economy and virtually no indigenous resources, to be nearly half self-sufficient with five new indigenous resources. In 1988 oil products accounted for 56 per cent of Denmark's energy consumption, electrical energy for 18 per cent, district heating for 13 per cent and natural gas for 7 per cent.

3.2   The transport system

3.2.1   *Transport development and policies*

The fundamental transport problems of Scandinavia have always been low overall population densities and the location of such exploitable natural resources as the forests of northern Sweden and the iron ore of Lapland at considerable distance from major cities and foreign markets. Kiruna, for instance, is 169 km inland and 1,900 km from Teesside and the Ruhr.

In the nineteenth century, Denmark, Norway and the northern Swedish forests were well placed to take advantage of steamship technology but railways were also necessary in order to link the cities and business centres and to enable inland regions to share national development. Experiments with private railways in Denmark and Sweden soon made it clear that only the State could borrow the foreign capital needed to build and operate a comprehensive inter-regional railway system.

The growth of road transport encouraged twentieth-century Scandinavian governments to invest heavily in roads during the 1950s and 1960s. At the same time rural depopulation resulted in one third of the population living in or near the four largest conurbations (see Table 1.1, p. 4). The transport problems of Scandinavia now developed three distinct dimensions: long intercity/inter-regional linkages; low rural demand for transport; and urban congestion (discussed in Chapter 4, section 4.3).

The maintenance of high living standards requires the major cities to have good road, rail and air interconnections and also links with the cities of the EC, Finland and, in the future, perhaps Warsaw, Leningrad and Moscow. Traffic between the cities is seldom sufficient to justify long stretches of motorway and double-track railway. On many routes there is hardly enough demand at present to justify competing road, rail and air services.

There has, however, been continuing pressure from business travellers for a wider network of air services, especially to the more isolated areas of northern Scandinavia and also for faster intercity trains. Regional policy also requires business people and civil servants to be able to attend meetings in major peripheral centres and to return to their headquarters within the day. Freight shippers also require faster, often smaller and more regular shipments as more and more production from scattered factories is integrated on the basis of 'just-in-time' deliveries. Road freight transport is much more flexible than rail in these respects.

Table 3.2 shows the demand for transport in Scandinavia. Despite the relatively high freight density, the relatively low intensity of use of the railway track emphasizes the cost of providing railway services. Ore from the Lapland mines to Narvik accounted for 21 per cent of all rail freight in 1987. Figure 3.3 shows the current pattern of railway passenger service to illustrate the present-day traffic pattern with its marked emphasis on intercity routes. Table 3.3 shows an average growth in Scandinavian passenger traffic (1960–88) of 9.5 per cent per annum and of freight traffic of 10.3 per cent per annum. Road traffic has grown steadily but rail traffic has fluctuated. Domestic air traffic has quadrupled since 1970. The current Nordic Economic Action Plan (Nordic Council

Table 3.2 The demand for transport, 1988

	Denmark	Norway	Sweden	Britain (1987)
Passenger km per head	12,700	11,800	12,400	10,700
Thousand tonne km per head	2,600	5,800	8,800	3,500
Million rail-traffic units per rail km*	2,753	1,130	2,163	3,384

* A traffic unit is a passenger km or a tonne km.
Sources: *Yearbook of Nordic Statistics* (1989–90); (British) *Annual Abstract of Statistic* (1988).

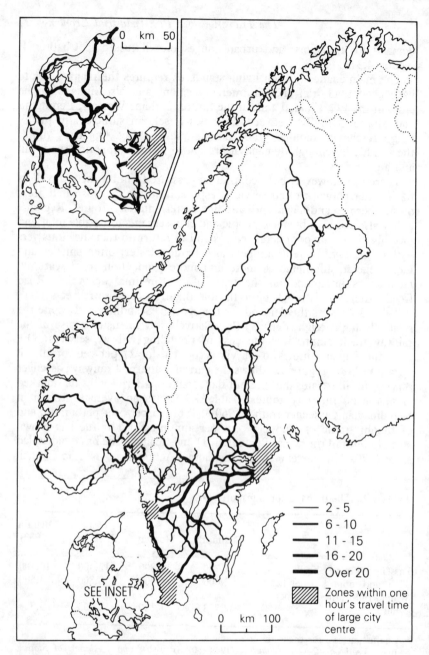

Figure 3.3 Railway passenger services, 1990

Table 3.3 Growth in Scandinavian traffic, 1960−88 (billions)

	1960	1970	1980	1988
Total passenger km	80.0	139.0	172	216
Road	52.0	108.0	154	195
Rail	10.0	9.0	15	15
Air★	0.3	1.5	3	6
(Of which public transport)			39	45
Total tonne km	38.0	74.0	80	92
Road	12.0	32.0	37	47
Rail	13.0	21.0	21	22
Sea★	9.0	19.0	22	23

★ Domestic traffic only.
Sources: *Yearbook of Nordic Statistics* (1989−90); *Transportarbeidet i Norden* (1980).

of Ministers, 1989) assumes that there will be increases in freight traffic at a rate of 3 per cent per annum and in passenger traffic at 4−5 per cent per annum through the 1990s, with most growth in longer journeys of over 300 km. Such increases, which might produce traffic volumes half as high again in 2000 as in 1990, would require difficult investment choices.

Table 3.4 shows the overall predominance of road transport, which carried 79 per cent of all Scandinavian traffic units (passenger km plus tonne km) in 1988. Car-ownership levels are high. In 1987 there were 2.4

Table 3.4 Modal share of traffic, 1988

	Denmark	**Norway**	**Sweden**
Billion passenger km			
Road	59.6	44.1	93.1
Rail	4.8	2.5	7.6
Air (domestic)	0.5	2.5	3.2
Billion tonne km			
Road	10.4	9.9	26.2
Rail	1.0	1.6	18.9
Sea (domestic)	2.0	13.0	7.9

Source: *Yearbook of Nordic Statistics* (1989−90).

persons per car in Sweden, 2.6 in Norway and 3.2 in Denmark (Britain 3.2). In Norway 85 per cent of households that include children own a car and almost half the journeys to work are made by car. Women have as good access to the use of a car as men in the Scandinavian countries. Increased expenditure on snow clearance and the improvement of roads to take higher axle loads has made road transport very competitive over short and medium distances where services such as door-to-door delivery may be as important as time or price. Since it may cost up to 40 per cent less to operate a ten-tonne truck than an eight-tonne truck, there is likely to be a further shift of traffic to roads from railways and coastal shipping by 2000. Combined road–rail services are being developed in order to combine the advantages of road and rail freight over longer distances.

With 86 per cent of the traffic growth recorded in Table 3.3 taking place on the roads, the original stringent regulation of transport competition on intercity routes has gradually broken down in favour of more expensive competitive services where the costs are shared between governments and traffic users. This process is by no means complete, since governments must still balance the advantages of sophisticated but under-used transport systems against the diversion of resources from other areas of expenditure, such as health and education.

Coastal shipping, which carried 25 per cent of Scandinavian tonne km in 1988, is generally a free market in Scandinavia. The role of competition in lowering the cost of imports and exports is widely accepted. Sea transport offers major price advantages for bulk goods but rapid delivery may be of equal importance for neo-bulk goods. Coastal shipping has lost virtually all journeys below 30 km to road haulage but offers some competition to road transport in the 30–150-km band and becomes significant in the (much smaller) markets for long-distance freight. In Norway, 75 per cent of freight moving more than 400 km goes by sea.

Regular Norwegian coastal shipping routes, which serve more than one county, are subject to State regulation of charges and services (which gives the government indirect power to rationalize services). Governments pay for the preservation of the fairways, lights, pilotage and ice-breaking. There is close international co-operation in the use of the Baltic ice-breakers between all the coastal states.

Internal air services offer increasing competition to the railways in Scandinavia because of the long distances between cities and the railway inheritance of lightly capitalized and somewhat circuitous routes, which make high speeds difficult to achieve. The current investment in a fixed link across the Great Belt and in faster intercity train services will reduce the competitive attraction of air travel within Denmark and southern Sweden. There has been a very cautious attitude to air-transport subsidy in all three countries. Even in north Norway, neither main routes nor air taxi services are subsidized, although the subsidies to short runway services to the islands and thinly populated mainland areas are arguably among the most important regional policies in Norway. Counties that demand more short airstrips than the State is prepared to supply must develop them out of their own resources. Competition between air and railway services is now essentially commercial in all three countries and there was a considerable rationalization of SAS services within Scandinavia in 1980. Air services do not rely solely on price competition with the railway since business travellers put a high value on their time. Both air and intercity railway services generally charge fares that cover their variable costs, but the substantially higher air fares contribute more to fixed costs than do railway fares.

Since the popular and ambitious road programmes of the 1960s were cut back during the economic crises of the 1970s, Scandinavian governments have been working towards criteria for transport investment that give the best return to the community as a whole rather than to any individual mode of transport. They have had to calculate the total social costs of transport, including those effects (such as noise and pollution) that cannot be priced by the market. Proposals for investment in roads and other facilities used by private transport should be compared with alternative investment in railways or sea transport. Public-transport fares and freight-transport charges should, as far as possible, reflect the extra costs the traffic imposes on the community.

Environmental concerns are playing an increasing role in transport policy. In the four large cities the car is increasingly seen as the enemy of a satisfactory urban environment and a variety of traffic-calming measures are being tried. Local authorities refuse to replace their urban fabric with motorways and, instead, are financing expensive public-transport alternatives. The three capitals have suburban railway networks, as has Århus. Stockholm has an extensive underground railway. Gothenburg relies on trams. In cities and counties alike, public transport is highly co-ordinated, with the railway stations acting as foci for the buses. The larger Scandinavian cities and all counties in Sweden offer relatively cheap monthly tickets that give unlimited access to the whole public-transport system. Stockholm is considering requiring car commuters to the inner city to buy a monthly public-transport ticket in order to discourage the use of the city's roads, while road-pricing schemes have been implemented in Oslo and Bergen. Norway has always taxed cars very highly, their purchase price has usually been twice as high as their declared import value.

Investment decisions, co-ordination of public transport and responsibility for setting fares on local transport have gradually been devolved from national governments to counties or to specially created transport authorities in the big cities (Fullerton, 1990). Heavily subsidized rural bus and taxi services provide reasonable levels of mobility for the less well-off and for non-car-owners. Buses also often carry post and parcels, which help to support their revenues. In parts of Norway and Sweden combined vehicles, part bus, part lorry, carry milk churns and other freight. Rural bus timetables are integrated with those of railways, car-ferry transport and coastal shipping, including the daily *hurtigruten* (coastal express steamer) between Bergen and Kirkenes, which calls at all inter-mediate ports. The integration of passenger transport improves through journey times, generates traffic and reduces the need for special school buses and social-welfare transport.

While social considerations play a major part in the transport policies of the county and city transport authorities, commercial criteria are judged more important for long-distance and national transport policies. Commercial criteria and the interests of the manufacturing industries (which underpin much of high Scandinavian living standards) would best be served by a close approximation to EC transport policies, the acceptance of the 40-tonne truck, the upgrading of roads in southern Scandinavia to carry them and a concentration of available transport investment on bridges and ferries to Germany. Such a policy would leave northern Scandinavia and most of Småland at a serious disadvantage in providing diversified employment for their people. The commitment of Scandinavian governments to equal opportunity for inhabitants of all regions of their countries requires them to assess the transport needs of different parts of the country in a way that differs considerably from that which would be brought about by market forces. While Conservative and Liberal Parties favour commercial investment criteria and Social Democrats are divided, the Centre, Christian, Left Socialist, Communist and Green Parties are more concerned with environmental and regional opportunity criteria. There is considerable and growing political opposition from left and centre parties in Norway and Sweden to the further construction of motorways and links to the EC. Social Democrats are divided. Com-promise and contradiction are therefore the order of the day in Scandinavian transport policy.

3.2.2 *Intercity transport*

As Scandinavia develops greater interchange of goods and people with the rest of Europe, both public and private transport operators are investing in the reduction of journey times and transport costs between the major Scandinavian cities and their European equivalents. It is Nordic Council policy to improve the main routes from Oslo, Stockholm and Copenhagen to Germany. The Council regards the transport infrastructure of central Sweden as adequate but sets out a number of priority areas for investment elsewhere, chiefly to improve access to the EC. It is planned to build longer motorway sections on the Oslo–Gothenburg–Copenhagen route, including a new bridge on the Norwegian–Swedish border and to double-track much of the railway. The Council also supports fixed links across the Øresund. Within Denmark, road and rail crossings of the Great Belt are under construction and are due to open in 1993 and 1996 respectively. The Danes intend to upgrade the road from Frederikshavn to the German border (an alternative route across Jutland for traffic from Norway and central Sweden to Germany) and to electrify the east-west railway between Copenhagen and Odense (on Fyn) by 1993. To balance this investment in access to and from the EC, the Nordic Council Economic Action Plan (Nordic Council of Ministers, 1989) also proposes investment in the transport systems of the Arctic North, notably in air transport to smaller settlements and in long-distance coach traffic.

Regular non-stop freight-train services from Scandinavian to mainland European termini began in 1989 and the national railway companies have joined with private road hauliers in the establishment of international combined road–rail services, such as containers, piggyback and trailer on train. Additional private railway ferries now link Gothenburg with Frederikshavn across the Kattegat, Malmö with Copenhagen across the Øresund and Trelleborg with Trävemunde across the Baltic.

Sweden has been in the forefront of the search for different solutions to the three distinct problems of intercity, urban and rural transport. In contrast to Denmark and Norway, railways were the mainstay of the Swedish inter-regional transport system until the 1950s. Road freight traffic was closely regulated from the 1920s in order to preserve the railway monopoly on long-distance transport and to avoid calls to upgrade thousands of kilometres of gravel-surfaced roads. After an exhaustive study of the Swedish transport system in 1961–3, road transport was gradually deregulated during the 1960s. At the same time competitive air-passenger services were introduced between Stockholm and the major regional centres.

In 1989, most of the Swedish railway track and stations were assigned to a National Rail Administration (Banverket). A similar State agency (Vägverket) is proposed for the trunk-road system. The same cost-benefit criteria are used to test proposals for investment in road and rail infrastructure. Swedish Rail (SJ) is now a commercial agency that provides passenger and freight services and pays Banverket for its use of railway track and terminals in proportion to traffic carried. County councils, using private contractors, also operate some rural rail services on Banverket, and other private operators may be admitted to the track in 1993.

SJ competes for freight with road hauliers and coastal shipping and with SAS and other airlines for long-distance passenger services. Long-distance coach services are not very well developed in Sweden. After forty years of limited investment in railway infrastructure (except for maintenance), a major investment plan was agreed in 1990 that will eventually allow speeds of 200 kph between Stockholm, Gothenburg and Malmö. SJ also works in partnership with private industry (notably the Swiss–Swedish firm, ASEA Brown-Boveri) in the building of rolling stock and with road hauliers in the provision and lease of container wagons and the establishment of combined road and rail freight services. The Swedish government pays for the preservation of unremunerative sleeper services to northern Sweden and contributes to the cost of the mainly iron-ore-carrying railway from Luleå to Narvik (whose future operation will be decided by a joint Norwegian–Swedish commission) and the inland railway from Gällivare to Lake Väner.

Land travel has always been difficult in Norway. There are still gaps served by ferries on each of the Oslo to Bergen roads and on the road to the Norwegian Arctic. Norway is still involved in primary road building, although to ever smaller and more isolated settlements. Norway shares with Switzerland the distinction of having the world's highest construction and maintenance costs for roads. Norwegian roads have light traffic but high maintenance costs of 37 NKr per metre as against 26–9 NKr per metre in Denmark and Sweden. Road expenditure is equally divided between investment and maintenance, with a continuing programme of road building accounting for 22 per cent of the trunk-road budget, 1990–3, and designed to substitute more direct land links for peripheral sea voyages and to replace ferries by bridges wherever feasible. Almost all trunk roads now have a hard surface and 80 per cent can carry 10-tonne trucks. However, only one fifth of the remaining (county) roads are built to this standard. Norway sees road building as an important element in regional policy, with 25 per cent of the 1990–3 regional development budget assigned to the North Norway Regional Programme and to a road in Vestfold. Road improvements in and around the cities of Oslo, Bergen and Trondheim are partially financed by tolls, since the Norwegian parliament has shown a preference for regulation of traffic through economic incentives rather than through compulsion, and is not prepared to earmark taxes for specific transport improvements.

In these circumstances Norwegian governments have been less enthusiastic about a market economy in intercity transport than have the governments of Denmark and Sweden. In 1973, the Norwegian government, in marked contrast to contemporary Swedish policy, declared Norwegian Railways (NSB) to be a community service in which commercial considerations were secondary: free customer choice must be subordinated to the total welfare of the economy. The Norwegian

Transport Act 1976 required road hauliers on regular routes to demonstrate the need for their service in order to obtain a licence. The licences included rather strict regulation of charges and frequency of services along the main highways, although hauliers had greater freedom of operation on the less-used roads. Goods-forwarding agents, who play a major role in Norwegian freight traffic, were obliged to use licensed hauliers on designated routes. The Ministry of Transport reserved powers to rationalize road-haulage businesses and to transfer their licences to county or municipal councils.

Railway development has been retarded by difficulties of terrain and shortage of traffic. Lines from Oslo only reached Bergen in 1909, Stavanger in 1944 and Bodø in 1962. Proposals to extend the northern line to Narvik and Tromsø face the prospect of very high costs and small revenues. There is very little traffic on intercity railways and only 6 per cent of traffic is now carried by rail. The closure of branch railway lines is resolutely opposed by local and regional interests. The proportion of railway costs covered by subsidy rose from 19 per cent to 30 per cent between 1970 and 1980. A new railway investment plan, gradually working towards speeds of 200 kph on main lines, was approved in 1989. In 1990 the Norwegian government took responsibility for the infrastructure cost of the railways with NSB accountable for the commercial operation of passenger and freight trains.

Denmark has the most liberal transport policies of the three countries, partly because, with nowhere in Denmark more than 60 km from a seaport, coastal transport has always been able to offer lively competition to road and rail. The Danish transport system is therefore essentially competitive, with road, rail and ferry transport handling the important international traffic between western Germany, Norway and Sweden on several routes. The Danish government and Danish local authorities became enthusiastic road builders during the 1960s and many new private ferry routes were established. Motorway enthusiasm waned in the 1970s but the basic framework of the Danish international railway system will be duplicated by motorways by the early 1990s. There are now a dozen major vehicle-ferry routes, six State railway ferry services and three private rail ferries across the Belts, the Øresund and the western Baltic.

Danish State Railways (DSB) is essentially an intercity/international system but has some long, rural, branch lines in Jutland and it operates suburban services in Copenhagen. DSB has traditionally drawn significant revenue from its car and truck ferries operating alongside the older rail–ferry routes. It has suffered from competition from the air services, which offer much faster travel between Copenhagen and Jutland. After 1993, however, the bridge and tunnel link across the Great Belt will enable much higher train speeds between Copenhagen, west Denmark and Hamburg, eventually leaving Ålborg as the only major Danish city with a faster centre-to-centre service to Copenhagen by air than by rail.

Government subsidies to the running and investment costs of DSB are steadily being reduced and the new business and express services that will be introduced when the Great Belt is bridged in 1993 will be required to cover their full costs. Environmental concerns are, however, increasingly compelling the Danish government to modify the tax system in order to encourage more people to use public transport and to transfer as much traffic as possible to rail.

The archipelagic nature of the country has so far prevented roads and railways developing their advantages of speed and bulk carriage. Land transport has overcome these barriers in three stages: the invention of rail ferries in the 1890s; the building of railway and road bridges across the narrower straits in the 1930s; and the current construction of bridges and tunnels from Sjælland across the Great Belt to Fyn.

An enabling Act for a bridge across the Great Belt in 1936 initiated a long political debate involving rival rail and road interests and the regional and planning problems of Jutland, Skåne and the Øresund conurbation focused on Copenhagen and Malmö. In 1988, contracts were signed for a Great Belt crossing avoiding the destruction of the environmentally sensitive island of Sprogø. An 8-km railway tunnel is being built from Halsskov (Sjælland) to Sprogø and a 6.6-km low-level rail/road bridge to Knudshoved (Fyn) should be finished by 1993. A 6.8-km high-level road bridge from Halskov to Sprogø will complete the road link in 1996. The crossing is being funded through international loans guaranteed by the Danish government and constructed by an international consortium. The cost will be paid off by user tolls until 2023. The number of cars crossing, which was 7,000 per day when construction began, is forecast to rise to 13,000 by 1996 as a result of general traffic growth, new traffic generated by the availability of the bridges and traffic diverted from the direct ferries now linking Jutland with Sjælland and southern Sweden. The railway freight traffic will be diverted to the Great Belt crossing from the present Copenhagen–Hamburg ferry route over the Fehmarn Belt, and the passenger-service time will be reduced from the present 5½ to 4½ hours by either route. It is believed that the crossing will save energy since ferries have a relatively high energy consumption and electric traction will eventually replace diesel operation on the railways.

It has long been appreciated that fixed links between Helsingør and Helsingborg, and Copenhagen and Malmö would complete the land linkage between Norway, Sweden and the rest of Europe and would also greatly improve local circulation for the two million inhabitants of the Øresund conurbation. Agreement on the type and location of fixed links has been delayed by similar rivalries of interest to those surrounding the

Great Belt crossing with the added complication of both Danish and Swedish interests to be considered. However, the Danes and Swedes have now agreed to build an 18-km bridge and tunnel link, carrying motorway and railway, from Copenhagen via Kastrup international airport to Malmö betwen 1993 and 2000. At a later date a railway tunnel may be built under the narrowest part of the Øresund from Helsingør to Helsingborg. A 21-km bridge across the Fehmarn Belt from Lolland to Germany is possible in the more distant future.

3.3 Manufacturing industries

3.3.1 The development of manufacturing

Remote from the main centres of European economic activity, with little capital, a poorly developed transport system and no local sources of energy other than wood, Scandinavia experienced what Pollard (1981) has called peripheral industrialization, which extended well into the twentieth century. In marked contrast to peripheral southern and eastern Europe, the Scandinavian countries were able to mobilize their managerial and political skills to compensate for the poverty of their natural resources. They had the initial advantages of a free peasantry and a good educational infrastructure. Foreign capital was essential in the early stages, especially for the building of the railways in advance of industrial demand, but it was important to prevent foreign lenders from determining the development of the Scandinavian economies. Foreign loans were therefore channelled through the national governments and only native companies were allowed to own land and the access to raw materials and water power that went with it. By these means Scandinavian firms and their bankers were left free to choose their own patterns of expansion and eventually to generate much of their own investment. Instead of becoming political and economic dependencies of the British and German empires, the Scandinavian countries developed as specialized but independent contributors to the western European economies with Danish agriculture, Norwegian hydro-electric technology and Swedish engineering becoming leaders in their field by the early twentieth century.

Native ores and local charcoal provided the bases for the first manufacturing industries. The Swedish firm, Stora, can trace its history back to the thirteenth century. Both Danish and Swedish governments actively encouraged foreign and native entrepreneurs to establish the iron, armaments and textile industries in the seventeenth century. Mead (1981), Jörberg (1973) and Jörberg and Krantz (1975) describe the rise of Scandinavian industry during the nineteenth and twentieth centuries. The sawmill industries of southern Norway and northern Sweden grew rapidly between 1870 and 1890 in order to meets the needs of the British market, but the long-established iron industry of central Sweden was forced to undergo the most drastic rationalization in competition with British and later German iron and steel industries. After 1890, engineering, paper and pulp industries were established as the economies of Norway and Sweden evolved from raw-material exports towards the sale of specialized finished goods. The Danes developed exports of semi-processed agricultural products, such as butter and bacon. Many but not all of the new factories located at the ports in order to receive seaborne coal from Britain and to reduce transport costs on their exports. At about the same time the development of hydro-electricity favoured the establishment of electro-metallurgical industries in remote Norwegian valleys and, when electricity transmission costs had come down, electrical engineering industries in central Sweden. A blossoming of Swedish inventive genius created new products and export opportunities including safety matches, ballbearings, the cream separator and gas accumulators.

The vertical integration of Scandinavian industry developed early, partly because the charcoal-iron and wood-processing industries both depended on timber as a raw material and on streams for water power. Several large firms emerged during the nineteenth century each owning a collection of mines, blast furnaces, rolling mills, iron foundries, metal workshops, sawmills and pulp factories. Export was essential in order to achieve a sufficient volume of production to tool up the factories. Many firms established subsidiaries abroad in order to avoid import duties and quotas, thereby laying the foundations of such well-known international Scandinavian firms as Ericsson, ASEA and SKF. The most technically advanced industries were found in or near the big five cities – Copenhagen, Stockholm, Oslo, Gothenburg, and Malmö – while traditional industries survived in a broad belt from the Oslofjord across Bergslagen to Stockholm and Gävle. Textile factories developed around Borås (in the hinterland of Gothenburg) and Norrköping. Glassworks were located in Småland. The industries of Swedish Norrland depended almost entirely upon forest products and there were several very isolated single-factory towns in the Norwegian valleys relying upon local hydro-electricity.

While the 1960s were a very prosperous decade for the Scandinavian economies as a whole, the manufacturing industries faced mounting problems in their export markets as world raw-material prices fell faster than other prices, and lower sea-transport costs on the new, large, bulk carriers brought ore from Brazil and Australia and wood pulp from North America into stronger competition with Scandinavian production on the European market. Apart from the Norwegian oil industry, there were few new factories based on indigenous raw materials.

Technical development enabled Western Europe and newly industrialized countries to catch up on some of the earlier Scandinavian lead in high-quality products. Newly industrialized countries had the additional advantage of lower labour costs. Scandinavian finished-steel and engineering products faced mounting Japanese competition. For clothing, textile and electrical goods the competition came from Korea, Taiwan and Singapore. By the mid-1960s all the major Scandinavian industries were fighting hard in foreign markets. The maintenance of free trade, which was essential if Scandinavian industry was to compete abroad, ensured that foreign competition was felt equally strongly in home markets.

During the oil crisis of 1973 and the subsequent industrial recession, Scandinavian industry continued to suffer from falling overseas markets for its exports while higher taxes and wages at home increased labour costs. The falling value of the dollar in relation to the krona sharpened North American competition in European markets. At the same time the cost of producing timber in Scandinavia rose rapidly in relation to production costs abroad. There was a steady fall in employment in manufacturing industry, most marked in textiles and clothing, transport equipment and construction materials.

In the early 1980s marked swings in the value of the dollar gave rise to unstable overseas markets for the forest-products industries. The relatively slow growth of the industrialized economies also imposed limited output. The Scandinavian countries reduced their trade barriers within EFTA and both Norway and Sweden have succeeded in reducing or abolishing many barriers to the entry of their goods into the EC market, at the expense of more foreign competition in their home markets.

Rising expenditure on research & development is characteristic of Scandinavian industry (Table 3.5), notably in Sweden, where it is often comparable in scale with outlay on plant and equipment. During the 1970s and 1980s technological ingenuity has been directed to reducing

Table 3.5 Expenditure on research & development as a percentage of GDP

	1981	1987 (est.)
Denmark	1.1	1.3
Norway	1.3	1.8
Sweden	2.3	3.1
West Germany	2.4	2.7
OECD	2.0	—

Sources: Nordic Council of Ministers (1989); OECD (1988–90).

the number of workers needed to achieve a given volume of production. Sweden has more industrialized robots per head than any other industrialized country. Corporation taxes allow very considerable deductions for investment and generally favour larger firms.

The co-existence of workshop industries capable of making components and large industrial assembly firms gives considerable flexibility to Scandinavian industrial production and allows a good spread of different kinds of work within each local employment area. Swedish firms are the chief organizers of flows of components.

Firms originally based on Scandinavian raw materials have used profits generated during upswings in demand to diversify their interests. Thus SCA (the Swedish Cellulose Association) bought Mölnlyke and Peaudouce, market leaders in hygiene products. Stora Kopparberg diversified out of iron and steel to buy Swedish Match, Papyrus and Billerud, a major forest-products complex. Engineering firms have also diversified through acquisitions − Electrolux into office equipment and Ericsson into computers.

Employers and trades unionists have generally agreed on policies favouring high productivity per worker, even if they lead to the contraction of the less competitive industries and encouraged the transfer of labour and capital to the more competitive. National wage agreements based on equal pay for equal work have facilitated the restructuring of industry in so far as national wage rates had to be paid irrespective of the profitability of individual industries or firms. The more profitable firms, notably in engineering and vehicle building, were able to pay lower wages than they might have had to in a free market and could use some of their profits to replace labour by capital equipment. In industries such as textiles and clothing, where the scope for rationalization was less, Scandinavian wages were maintained well above those of their international competitors and imports rapidly replaced home production.

The high value placed on productivity, together with legislation that codified rights related to dismissal and redundancy, put union representatives on the boards of private companies and expanded industrial retraining schemes, allowed some industries to contract with less associated structural unemployment and social protest than in much of Western Europe.

As international trade has grown, production has specialized, but the relative advantages of particular locations have, in many cases, diminished. Törnqvist (1986) points out that transport costs have fallen relative to labour and warehousing costs and their significance in the location of industry has thereby diminished. Larger production and assembly plants have been built in order to achieve the economies of scale needed to meet foreign competition. These changes have increased the amount of transport undertaken as assembly plants are able to look further afield − to other Scandinavian countries and abroad − for their component suppliers.

Industries engaged in high-value export production, where labour costs outweigh the costs of assembly of raw materials, have a fair degree of freedom of location. This often means that they are free to stay where they are, adjusting changes in production at the existing site or developing the site and its labour supply to meet changing production demands. A slow dispersion of manufacturing industry from the major cities began during the Second World War as firms looked for cheaper sites and new (possibly more adaptable) labour forces. In Denmark, Copenhagen had 48 per cent of all industrial workers in 1958 but only 24 per cent by 1980. By the early 1980s, two thirds of the workers in Swedish manufacturing industry were employed in essentially footloose industries. This outward movement was helped by regional aid policies from the 1960s onwards. As elsewhere, Scandinavian branch plants have often concentrated on standardized and routine sectors of the production process.

3.3.2 The organization of production and investment

There is a marked concentration of industrial decision-making in Scandinavia with a complex web of cross-ownership of voting shares between firms. In Sweden the twenty largest companies employ 40 per cent of the industrial workforce and almost all are associated with one or other of two investment groups, each linked to a major bank: the Volvo-Skanska group includes Euroc, Opus, Pharmacia, Sandvik, Skanska and Volvo, while Asea-BB, Astra, Atlas-Copco, Electrolux, Ericsson, Saab-Scania, SKF, Stora and Swedish Match are in the Wallenberg group. Tax law favours the institutional ownership of firms. Foreigners have so far had very limited access to voting shares but if Norway or Sweden were to enter the EC or further harmonize their financial practices with those of the EC, such severe restrictions on foreign ownership would be difficult to sustain and national control of major firms might be threatened. The exchange of voting shares between Volvo and Renault in 1990 foreshadows such changes.

As major sources of capital, the banks have a strong influence on the location of factories, generally favouring the expansion of existing efficient plants and the closure of the less efficient rather than substantial relocation of industry. Governments, on the other hand, are more concerned about the social costs of closure and the extent of local industrial diversification so, while reluctant to see the closure of works that dominate a local employment area, they have often been willing to encourage other industries to come in and provide alternative employment.

Relatively few firms are owned by the State in Scandinavia – only 10 per cent of the total in Sweden, for instance. Some of these are directly responsible to a ministry, such as the Danish and Norwegian State Railways. Others, like ASSI (Swedish National Forest Industries) and Statoil, which operates the Norwegian sector of the North Sea oilfields, are semi-independent agencies with the State exercising arms-length control through its shareholdings. The Norwegian government has a controlling interest in Norsk Hydro. Government influence on manufacturing firms (notably Bofors and Saab-Scania) may also be exercised through defence procurements. Regional policies no longer include direct pressure on firms to locate at specific places.

The process of privatization may be illustrated by the firm Procordia (originally known as Statsföretag) which was established in 1970 to invest the income of the Swedish State Pension Fund. Under the centre-right governments of 1976–82, Statsföretag bought interests and negotiated rationalizations in a number of ailing manufacturing industries including 67 per cent of SSAB (Swedish Steel) and 40 per cent of Södraskogägarna (a forest-exploiting co-operative) and control of the remainder of the shipbuilding industry (now called Celsius Industries). Under Social Democratic governments, Procordia has sold several of its home interests in manufacturing industry (including Swedish Steel) to private insurance and pension funds and bought into hotel and entertainment enterprises. Procordia has substantially increased its holdings abroad (in such firms as Coventry Climax).

There has been an increase in the size of industrial plant. In Sweden, fifteen firms now employ 40 per cent of the industrial workforce. Amalgamations and take-overs have taken place in order to control or 'stabilize' a greater part of the market or to take advantage of tax concessions or (most commonly) to offer stronger competition in foreign markets. Combination into larger firms may provide greater security for particular factories but decision-making moves ever upwards to the larger cities.

The growing integration of production and exchange among the developed countries of the world is of increasing importance to Scandinavia. The ten largest Swedish companies account for one third of Swedish exports and Swedish multinationals employ over half of all the Swedish workers in factories of over 50 employees (a further 7 per cent are employed by foreign multinationals). Ownership is somewhat less concentrated in Denmark and Norway. The ten largest Swedish firms contribute 33 per cent of the value added by manufacturing industry, the ten largest Norwegian firms 23 per cent and the Danish top ten 13 per cent. Small Danish firms often sell their products to larger firms that are well established in foreign markets. There is little direct foreign investment in Danish manufacturing although there have been substantial foreign loans negotiated through Danish banks.

Scandinavian firms began establishing plants abroad before the First World War but the internationalization of business began to develop on a large scale during the 1960s. There was often a step-by-step process led on by the need for Scandinavian producers to add as high a value as possible to their products. As home markets are small they must seek wider markets abroad in order to cover research, development and other fixed costs and to purchase high-quality materials. Many Scandinavian firms established a network of sales agents abroad but as soon as rising sales justified the expense, they would develop their own foreign sales organization. If this led to further expansion of sales abroad, firms would set up factories there, combining expensive research & development in Scandinavia with the lower production costs often found in other countries. Manufacture in branch plants abroad enabled firms to avoid external tariffs, reduce transportation costs and make closer physical contact with major foreign markets. The thirty largest Swedish companies earn 60 per cent of their profits abroad. Swedish firms and their subsidiaries employed about 400,000 workers abroad by 1989. Volvo employed 30 per cent of its workers abroad and Electrolux 79 per cent. SKF is truly multinational, employing over half its workers abroad to manufacture four fifths of its products. Only 5 per cent of its goods are sold in Sweden.

With higher returns on foreign investments than are available at home and the approach of the single European market of 1993, Swedish firms have been actively investing in and buying EC firms. They invested more abroad than at home in 1989 and, during the first half of 1990, led the world in the amount spent on the acquisition of EC firms. Meanwhile Statoil was actively pursuing joint exploration projects with foreign oil companies.

Foreign investment in the Scandinavian countries is on a much smaller scale. In 1990 Swedish investment in the EC amounted to 46 billion SKr but EC investment in Sweden was only 5 billion SKr. The Scandinavian home markets are too small and scattered to justify the attentions of the larger multinational corporations but mergers with medium-sized Finnish and Swiss firms have resulted in 200,000 employees of foreign or jointly owned firms. In the motor-vehicle industry, where effective competition on world markets requires a scale of operation beyond the resources of small countries, General Motors bought a 50-per-cent share in the car division of Saab-Scania in 1989; Volvo and Renault exchanged significant quantities of shares in 1990.

Like foreign trade, Scandinavian investment and employment is heavily concentrated in developed countries. Of Swedish investment abroad in 1990, 25 per cent was in Norway, 5 per cent in other northern countries,

22 per cent in Britain, France and West Germany, 20 per cent in the USA and only 13 per cent in Third World countries. Similarly, 44 per cent of the overseas employees of Swedish firms worked in the EC and 30 per cent were in other OECD countries. Some less developed countries have welcomed the know-how Scandinavian firms can bring to infant industries. Some Scandinavian firms have bought exploitation rights to raw materials in Third World countries, such as Liberian iron ore.

As a typical example of a large Swedish firm, Volvo has 79,000 workers, of which 56,000 work in Sweden, with another 12,000 Swedish workers (and many more abroad) engaged on subcontracts. The firm began as a downstream development from SKF ballbearings, beginning with the manufacture of cars in 1927. Eventually Volvo bought up a number of its original component suppliers and now manufactures almost two thirds of the value of its own vehicles. Volvo's initial strategy was to build 'winterized' cars for the home market but later began to sell cars to countries that did not manufacture their own. In the 1950s Volvo began to penetrate the North American and West European markets and set up its first assembly plant abroad in 1965. By 1989, Volvo supplied 15 per cent of the EC and 12 per cent of the USA truck markets. During the 1970s Volvo entered into co-operative production agreements with several major, foreign, car manufacturers, culminating in a large investment in Renault in 1990. By purchasing the Dutch vehicle builder, Daf, and the British Leyland Bus, Volvo became a significant producer within the EC. Today Volvo has 1,565 direct suppliers (often themselves relying upon components from other firms) of whom 853 are in Sweden, 70 in Denmark and Norway, 260 in Britain, 192 in North America and most of the remainder in the other EEC countries. In addition to its motor-vehicle output, Volvo has diversified into other branches of engineering (including aero-engines for Saab). Volvo's shareholding in Procordia — a group of formerly State-owned companies — equalled that of the Swedish government by 1990.

3.3.3 The metal and engineering industries

The steel industry is central to metal and engineering output. Production rose from 1.7 million tonnes in 1950 to 6.8 million in 1970 but subsequently fell to 5.5 million tonnes by 1988. While crude steel is imported, Scandinavian steelmakers have sought to add value by concentrating on the production of 'special' steels containing valuable alloys and usually made to customer's specification. The market value of these steels (including stainless steel) may be up to three times the value of crude steel. Special steels account for 30 per cent of Swedish steel output but 60 per cent of the employment and the value added.

Most steelworks form relatively small but vital divisions of larger firms. Co-operation between these firms enables each to specialize and there are considerable financial linkages between them. Small quantities of steel are made in foundry works at Stavanger, Oslo and Copenhagen and in scrap-based works at Halmstad, Källinge and Gullspäng. Three coastal steelworks (at Öxelösund and Luleå in Sweden and at Mo i Rana in Norway) were built after the Second World War in order to take advantage of lower freight charges on coal, iron ore and scrap steel. Luleå and Mo i Rana were intended to become cornerstones for regional industrialization (see Chapter 5, section 5.5).

With four fifths of Scandinavian steel fabricated into investment goods, the industry is very sensitive to fluctuations in international demand and also suffered in the 1970s when unit labour costs rose 18 per cent faster than those of its competitors. As foreign markets contracted there was decline in the shipbuilding, metalworking and construction industries at home. The Norwegian and Swedish governments sought to subsidize and restructure the steel industry but eventually commercial considerations were allowed to determine the re-organization of the Swedish special-steel industry. Only steelworks that were able to integrate their production with downstream metalworks survived this crisis. The labour force fell from 58,000 in 1977 to 47,000 in 1987. However, productivity had risen and output was concentrated on technically advanced steels. Half the steel is produced by electric furnaces, half in LD (oxygen using) convertors. Scrap has become the main raw material of the industry with the only blast furnaces remaining at Luleå and Öxelösund. Mo i Rana switched from Norwegian coal and iron to scrap.

Aluminium smelting developed into a major Norwegian industry during the industrial expansion of the 1960s. Using cheap hydro-electricity, the Norwegian government was able to attract North American producers into partnerships and four major smelters were built on the Norwegian coast between 1958 and 1971.

The engineering and vehicle-building industries have quadrupled output over the last twenty years. In 1986 the engineering and vehicle-building industries accounted for one third of all employment in Scandinavian manufacturing industries. Half their output (in terms of value) is exported and engineering products comprise half of all Swedish exports. With Electrolux as the world's largest supplier of household appliances and Asea Brown-Boveri (the Swiss Swedish consortium) the world's largest heavy electrical firm, seven of Sweden's top-ten companies are world leaders in their product range.

There has been a growing financial integration within these industries as production has become more sophisticated. The large internationally known companies, such as Alfa-Laval, Asea, Atlas-Copco, Electrolux,

Ericsson, Saab-Scania, SKF and Volvo, are all involved in a variety of engineering production at several plants. Since the Second World War component works have been established in inland areas either in search of labour or encouraged thither in order to diversify the local industrial structure. Assembly plants have been located on coastal or near-coastal sites in order to import components and export their finished products more easily. As a result, the distribution of employment in engineering and vehicle building is widespread in central and southern Scandinavia and there are important outposts near the larger towns in northern Sweden.

High-technology production is more closely concentrated into an area within 150 km of Stockholm. The city has one third of its manufacturing industry employees in occupations related to technological skill and research & development. This is partly because technical change in Scandinavia employs many imported techniques and Stockholm has the most contacts with the world outside, and partly because a number of the large companies that undertake most of the research & development have head offices there. Important exceptions include Ludvika, 180 km north west of Stockholm, where Asea-Brown Boveri has Scandinavia's most advanced laboratory for power transmission, and Umeå, 500 km north of Stockholm, which is developing into a major centre of research into computer technology. It is Swedish government policy to establish so-called K-regions (K for know-how) focused upon provincial universities and technical colleges.

The motor-vehicle industry, with its assembly plants in western Sweden, has grown steadily since the Second World War and, by the late 1980s, was creating half of the new jobs in Swedish manufacturing industry. In 1986 Sweden produced 421,000 cars, of which 80 per cent were exported, accounting for 15 per cent of Swedish exports. Although facing fierce competition from Germany and Japan in the medium-to-large car market, Sweden holds a significant share of the European heavy and medium truck market and 90 per cent of trucks were exported in 1986.

The largest vehicle assembly plants are at Gothenburg and nearby Trollhättan. Expanding output during the 1970s enabled Volvo to establish six new branch plants, of which four are within 150 km of Gothenburg. The Kalmar assembly plant (1974) has substituted working groups for the traditional assembly lines. Increased flexibility of production and the economic possibility of profitability on shorter runs of cars has made contact with component suppliers more critical and may lead to a further geographical concentration of component manufacture within relatively short distances of Gothenburg.

Exports are particularly important for the machinery and machine-tool branches of engineering, especially pulp and paper machinery, pumps and workbench tools. All these products are very sensitive to fluctuations in foreign demand and the relatively high costs of Scandinavian production. Electrical-engineering exports have shown marked recent growth. Computer-equipment manufacture is linked to several sectors of the engineering industry and represents perhaps 10 per cent of the industrial output of Sweden. The importance of foreign firms in data-processing helps to explain the concentration of production in the northern suburbs of Stockholm, where foreign firms started as selling agencies but later established production.

Many Scandinavian electrical firms were originally based on the availability of cheap hydro-electric power and the later development of its transmission over long distances to Oslo and southern Sweden. The industry is dominated by such large firms as ASEA, Ericsson and Electrolux, with half of their workforces employed in foreign branch plants or subsidiaries. Electrolux, the largest manufacturer of 'white goods' in the world, owns plants in ten EC countries and employs one third of its staff there. Sweden also participates in the European Space Agency. One third of the employment is in the Stockholm area but smaller units are widespread.

In pursuance of Sweden's policy of armed neutrality, defence equipment is manufactured at home, providing a market for sophisticated electronics. Sweden spends more per head on armaments than any other Northern or Western European country. It is also the only country outside NATO and the Soviet Union that produces submarines and supersonic jet aircraft and also manufactures heavy artillery, light tanks and missiles. Sweden's arms producers sell the bulk of their output to their own government but are also major exporters in order to keep the economies of scale necessary to ensure an adequate and economic supply of equipment to the Swedish defence forces. Although Swedish firms are not allowed to sell arms to countries actually at war, the threat of war preserves many markets in the Third World and some breaches of official policy on arms sales to combatants have come to light in recent years. The extent to which the industry will lose markets as a result of the ending of the Cold War remains to be seen.

3.3.4 The forest-products and chemical industries

The forest-products industries produce roundwood, pulp and paper in widespread factories that provide valuable small-scale manufacturing employment in many rural areas. Scandinavia, together with Finland, produces four times as much paper as it uses so is very vulnerable to changing world markets. Having pioneered the technical development of the pulp and paper industries, the Scandinavians found themselves in the 1960s with plant that was often smaller scale than that built at a later date in Finland and North America. Since the 1960s the forest-products industries have faced rather large cyclical swings in world demand and increasing competition from overseas producers. Technical developments in the 1950s and 1960s widened the range of hardwood trees available for the economic production of wood pulp. These developments reduced the comparative advantages of the Scandinavian softwoods relative to domestic hardwood production in western Europe. Norway and Denmark were already net importers of timber. Scandinavian producers were forced to rationalize, closing many of the older sulphite paper and pulp plants and the smaller sawmills.

Many forest-products firms hold substantial assets in the form of forest land and hydro-electric power resources, which help them to ride out fluctuations on the timber market. Scandinavian producers have compensated for their higher raw material costs by concentrating production on the more expensive grades of paper and by using the profits generated during periods of high demand to diversify into consumer products and to invest abroad. Rationalization improved productivity per worker during the 1960s but a short-lived revival in the fortunes of the industry was abruptly halted by the oil crisis of 1973.

About half of the cut timber is processed in Scandinavian sawmills and marketed in the building and furniture industries and in the West European building industry. Sawmills are scattered across the whole forested zone of Norway and Sweden. While most are small, they account for a significant number of jobs in their local economies. In Swedish Inner Norrland, for instance, sawmilling accounts for half the employment in manufacturing industries. While the northern forests of Sweden are dominated by sawmills owned by large companies, each producing a wide range of products (including Stora — Europe's largest forest-products firm), most of the sawmills in southern Sweden are independent, buying their timber from the local farmers. There has been a long-term trend southwards where trees grow more rapidly and in a greater variety of species.

The manufacture of furniture, prefabricated housing and sports equipment is widely spread. Export markets have been created by the success of Scandinavian designers in penetrating the sophisticated markets of West Europe and North America. The furniture industry, for example, is established in many small towns and villages in Jutland and west Norway and lends itself to small-firm organization where enterprise and design flair are more important locating factors than access to capital or raw materials. Diversification from wood into plastics in the early 1950s eventually enabled Lego at Billund to become Europe's largest toy manufacturer, while Bang & Olufsen, another village enterprise, diversified into high-fidelity radio and television.

Half of the cut timber goes direct into the pulp and paper mills (which also receive about a quarter of their raw material as offcuts from sawmills). Sweden exports 90 per cent of the market pulp produced. The replacement of timber floating by the faster and more flexible road transport reduced the locational advantages of river-mouth sites for the principal wood-processing plants in favour of inland sites with a larger hinterland within the same radius. At the same time, the increasing carriage of timber by sea in bulk carriers concentrated international traffic into a small number of deep-water ports at which the timber brought by road or coastal steamer had to be transhipped. Sweden exports 75 per cent of output of paper and board. Rationalization has drastically reduced the number of pulp mills but those remaining are very large and often integrated with paper mills. Unlike the saw mills, pulp mills are restricted to coastal or lakeside locations because of the pollution they cause. Pollution has, in fact, been drastically reduced during the 1970s and 1980s with 10–15 per cent of total investment in the pulp and paper industry being devoted to environmental protection measures. Pulp mills are found along the Bothnian and Baltic coasts of Sweden and around Oslofjord.

Paper mills are more widely scattered than pulp mills and more are found inland. The large forest-product companies of northern Sweden and Norway have invested in Portugal and Canada rather than in southern Sweden where SIAB, a farmer/forester co-operative centred on Växsjö, has plant at Mönsterås, Mörrum and Värö.

Oil provides the basis for most industries established since the Second World War. Petrochemicals are not developed on a large scale since it is difficult to reap the economies of scale available at Rotterdam or on Teesside. The chief refineries, on the Skaggerak, each have an associated petrochemical industry. Many of the Scandinavian chemical plants are owned by firms whose prime interest is in metallurgy or forest products. In chemicals, as elsewhere, Scandinavian production tends towards fine and speciality chemicals. Other chemical production is associated with large integrated pulp and paper mills, as at Borregaard, near the Oslofjord and with major steelworks. Norsk Hydro has a large electrochemical complex at Herøya, near Skien, using imported raw materials and magnesite from the sea to produce fertilizers and a range of other chemicals. Power was obtained from the Eidfjord, and raw materials, including bauxite, imported directly. The end-products are aluminium, magnesium, polyvinyl chloride and polyethyline. Norsk Hydro supplies a considerable part of the whole Scandinavian market for fertilizers. The main petro-chemical investment of the 1970s was the Norsk Hydro plant at Mongstad (Figure 3.1), which exchanges some products with the Herøya complex.

The Norwegian electrochemical industry grew up at the beginning of the twentieth century when electricity transmission costs were very high and hydro-electric power was relatively cheap at some isolated valley and fjordhead sites. Eventually the cheap electricity in the mountains ceased to compensate for the costs of bringing the raw materials up from the coast. Rjukan and Notodden converted to the manufacture of liquid ammonia.

The Swedish chemical industry has a fairly wide range of products. It includes the manufacture of phosphate fertilizers, sulphuric acid and other inorganic chemicals and bleaches for the pulp and paper industry. The industry is largely based on inventions in the field of explosives, safety matches and plastics. There is a synthetic chemical industry (originally based on ethyl alcohol from the pulp industry) associated with the refinery at Stenungsund. The pharmaceutical chemical industry is growing rapidly with research & development costs equivalent to 30 per cent of value added. The largest plant is at Södertälje and much of the production is exported. The Danish chemical industry also concentrates on pharmaceutical products. There is a large fertilizer plant at Danfoss in Als.

3.3.5   The decline of shipbuilding and textiles

The failure of some manufacturing industries to maintain their position in an increasingly competitive world market has not been due to poor organization, low investment or lack of technological development. The Scandinavian shipbuilding industry took full advantage in the high demand for new ships during the economic boom of the 1950s and 1960s. Norwegian shipowners, in particular, disappointed by uncertain deliveries from British yards, turned to the shipyards of Uddevalla, Gothenburg, Malmö, Odense and Copenhagen, which were extensively modernized at that time. Smaller yards at Ålborg, Frederiksværk and Helsingør in Denmark and also in southern Norway built for the growing ferry market. Several yards followed the trend to large, simple, bulk carriers and high-quality purpose-built ships, both incorporating the latest marine technology. Kockums yard at Malmö was designed to launch bulk carriers of up to 500,000 DWT; the Arendal yard (1963), downstream from Gothenburg, pioneered wholly new techniques of assembly-line indoor construction. In the 1950s and 1960s, when world freight-shipping capacity was growing at a rate of 8 per cent per annum to meet a growth of tonne mileage of over 12 per cent per annum, Scandinavian yards were building 10 per cent of world output. Production peaked in 1976 when Sweden alone built 2.9 million tonnes. There were then six large yards in Sweden employing 26,500 men and six yards in Denmark, employing

19,000 out of a total of 25,000. Several of these yards were the dominant employers in their communities, notably at Uddevalla, north of Gothenburg, and at Nakskov on the otherwise agricultural island of Lolland. Shipbuilding accounted for 25 per cent of the diverse manufacturing labour force of Gothenburg.

During the industrial crisis of the mid-1970s, large amounts of world tonnage were laid up and order books emptied. The rationalization and closure of yards did not follow long-term plans but was the result of the responses of owners, managements, unions and governments to a series of month-to-month crises. When the oil crisis of 1973 began, order books were full and, as they emptied, the Norwegian and Swedish governments gave substantial subsidies to their shipbuilding industries. Between 1976 and 1982 the Swedish subsidy bill amounted to 320,000 SKr per employee (as opposed to only 21,000 SKr per employee for textile workers). The Swedish yards were nationalized in 1977 and then closed one by one from 1979 until 1986. The Arendal yard switched from shipbuilding to ship-repairing in 1978 and has since turned to the building of offshore oil rigs. Only in 1983 was everyone concerned reconciled to a major contraction of the shipbuilding industry in Denmark and Norway and to its virtual disappearance from Sweden (Strath, 1987). Two of the closed Swedish yards have been replaced by car-assembly plants.

The Danish government did not subsidize shipbuilding but allowed a system of leaseback and loans as profitable tax-avoidance schemes for investors, thus helping the industry as a whole rather than individual shipyards. The Burmeister & Wain shipyard near Copenhagen, after five years of contraction under the management of a wealthy idiosyncratic entrepreneur, was virtually nationalized in 1980. Shipbuilding ceased at Helsingør but repair work continues. The Nakskov shipyard was retained as it was the only large industrial employer in the area.

Textiles and clothing have also been in decline after considerable post-war expansion. The world textile industry has grown more slowly than other manufacturing industries with the centrally controlled economies and Third World countries supplying more of the market. Competition from low-cost producers has severely affected the Scandinavian textile and clothing industries. In the Borås district of Sweden alone, employment fell from 43,000 in 1970 to 19,000 in 1985.

The remaining clothing enterprises, supported by regional development aid, have moved upmarket. At the same time Scandinavian firms have established branches in Britain, Portugal, Finland and elsewhere, putting out the sewing work abroad but retaining design, market development and administration at home. As the industry has contracted, several of the more recent firms in Stockholm, Malmö and Norrköping have closed, leaving the industry more concentrated in its traditional home around

Borås. The Danish textile and clothing industries have a similar concentration around Ikast and Herning in western Jutland. By the end of the 1980s, however, both the textile and clothing industries in Scandinavia began to increase production volume again and also made substantial improvements in productivity.

3.4   The developing service economy

High living standards and sophisticated production require an extensive array of services. These may be usefully grouped into producer services, which provide inputs to the production of other enterprises, distributive and transport services, social services, which are delivered to people in respect of their perceived needs and personal services, which individuals buy according to their own inclinations and wealth.

Figure 3.4 shows the growth of service employment in Scandinavia. This trend is broadly comparable (as far as differences in international classification allow) to that in other developed Western countries. Employment in producer and social services, notably financial, educational and health services, increased very rapidly during the 1960s and 1970s. During the 1980s, however, the rate of growth in public services declined steadily. In Sweden, for instance, public-service employment was growing at 4.5 per cent annually, 1975–81, but slowed to 0.9 per cent in 1982–7. Employment in personal services showed moderate growth during the 1980s. Distributive and transport services raised productivity but not employment.

The growth of telecommunications is facilitating the concentration of producer services into the larger cities and thereby separating workers in these services from many of their customers. Most social and distributive services and many personal services, including tourism, still require the supplier and user of the service to be in at least temporary personal contact at the same place. The growth of employment in social services, which the customer receives by right, therefore reinforces the existing distribution of population except in so far as the services can be supplied in a local service centre the customer can visit. All over Scandinavia public services are concentrated at county towns and municipal centres where administrative offices, regional offices of ministries and national agencies, general hospitals and high schools are found. Half of the Swedish budget for higher education and research is spent in the large cities.

While employment in retailing broadly follows the distribution of population, the retail trades have been rationalized during the last thirty years as small- and medium-sized shops in towns were replaced by hypermarkets, supermarkets and more specialized shops. All but the

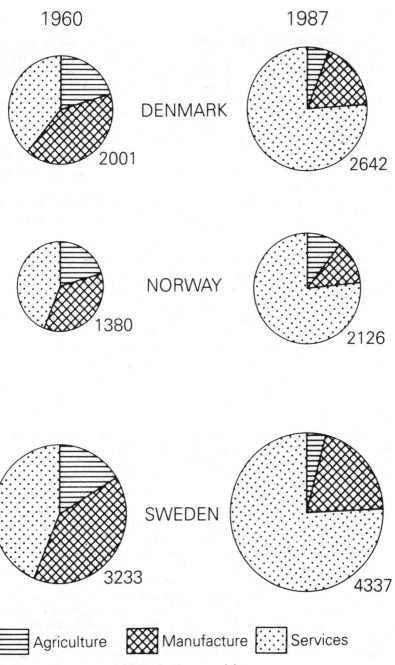

1960	1987

DENMARK

2001   2642

NORWAY

1380   2126

SWEDEN

3233   4337

▦ Agriculture   ▨ Manufacture   ⋰ Services

Figures refer to workforce (in thousands)

Figure 3.4 Occupational structure, 1960 and 1987

largest variety stores and the smallest local groceries are self-service. The co-operative movement is very strong in Scandinavia and many independent traders have banded together in order to enjoy similar economies of scale in production and distribution of their supplies. The concentration of services has proved a particular problem in Norway, where the consolidation of communes into municipalities of a viable size for efficient service provision threatens the inhabitants of many scattered and isolated settlements with unacceptably long and difficult journeys to shops, schools and doctors. Several of the larger municipalities have two or more service centres and the national government subsidizes the operation of local daily needs shops.

Personal services depend to a greater extent upon the distribution and concentration of wealth and have, together with producer services, grown most rapidly in the capital cities, which not only act as the leading centres for the reception of international contacts and innovations from abroad but are also the hubs of domestic transport and communication systems. Scandinavian capitals also attract career-oriented people in all branches of service industry and are widely regarded as the most interesting places to work. The three capital cities, together with Gothenburg, Malmö and Århus, account for two thirds of wholesale employment and over one half of workers in banking and financial services. In 1985 private services employed 44 per cent of the workforce in the Stockholm region, 38 per cent in Gothenburg, but only 29 per cent in Northern Norrland and 15 per cent in Inland Norrland. Private services have supplied half of the employment growth in Greater Stockholm during the 1980s and are forecast to provide half of all new jobs in Sweden up to 1995.

With four to five weeks guaranteed annual holiday for all workers, tourism plays a significant role in local Scandinavian economies. Its impact is widespread and there are no sizeable single-industry resorts. Tourism provides extra income in many mountain valleys and contributes significantly to the revenues of the Coastal Express shipping route (*hurtigruten*) along the Norwegian coast and the ferries in and around the Danish archipelago. While young Scandinavians take the opportunity to travel widely, many families take a tropical or Mediterranean holiday during the winter followed by a longer touring holiday within Scandinavia during the summer, also making frequent trips to their summer cottage. This pattern results in a debit balance on the officially recorded income and expenditure of tourists, which amounted to US$4,572 million in 1987 (*Yearbook of Nordic Statistics*, 1988). High living costs discourage foreign visitors to Scandinavia despite the well-known attractions of the Norwegian fjords and the less well-known attractions of the Swedish and Danish summer climate. The division of Germany from 1945 until 1990 gave West Germany a very restricted sea coast and encouraged large numbers of Germans to visit the beaches of west Jutland. The spread of German summer tourism has so far been held in check by prohibitions on foreign ownership of summer houses or other property.

A large public sector is one of the characteristic features of the Scandinavian economies (see Table 1.2, p. 15). Public services employ about one third of the entire Scandinavian workforce and their wages account for half of all public expenditure. The scale and pattern of supply of services is, however, not significantly different from that in the USA, where many services that are public in Scandinavia are offered through the private sector. Most welfare in Scandinavia is provided by local government or community agencies working to State guidelines. The national civil service is restricted to ministries, State agencies, higher education and defence. There is very little private education or medicine and almost all the clergy are State servants. State agencies provide most of the public transport and communication. The growth of local-authority employment reflects the rapid recent growth of health services, especially for the elderly and handicapped. Although these large public-service sectors are regulated and sheltered from the disciplines of the market, their labour requirements can push wages up and so fuel inflation. The Scandinavian right-wing parties argue that the high public spending and taxation necessitated by the size of the public-service sector weakens the incentive to private saving and may encourage too many people to work in the 'sheltered' sectors of the economy.

Competition with the private sector is not the only way to increase public-sector productivity. Many productivity gains have been made through the structuring of government grants to public agencies and local authorities so as to enforce the necessary economies. Danish grants to local government, for instance, are related to local tax income and specific local needs while central government budgets assume an annual gain in productivity of 2.5 per cent. The total public-sector wage bill was cut by 3 per cent in 1989. Similar linkage of appropriations to improvements in productivity have been made in the Norwegian and Swedish budgets.

By the mid-1980s, 80 per cent of local-government employees in Sweden were women and 56 per cent worked part time (Törnqvist, 1986). The expansion of the service sector through the recruitment of women, most of whom work part time, has been facilitated by generous maternity (and paternity) leave and subsidies to day-care nurseries. Part-time work is a major source of family income and enables governments to influence the distribution of service employment and earnings in the interests of regional policy. In 1972 the Swedish parliament decreed that people all over the country should, as far as possible, have a similar range of work opportunities. The government has dispersed many ministerial and State-agency employees from Stockholm to regional capitals and other provincial towns. The five northernmost counties of Norway and Sweden have more than their fair share of public employment as a result of vigorous regional policies and a concentration of defence services near the Finnish frontier. Defence spending in these areas may, however, be reduced in the future with the ending of the Cold War. In the northern half of Sweden (north of 62°) more people are employed in the caring services and education than in the raw-material-based industries. During the 1980s prosperity in this area has been confined to major service centres where most of the employment is sheltered from the vicissitudes of the international economy. Any downturn in the international economy would accentuate these disparities between the larger service centres and the industrial towns and remoter rural areas.

This chapter has discussed the processes of industrial change. While the increased participation of women in the labour force and the stagnation or decline in male employment in agriculture and manufacturing industry have been dominant themes in most developed countries, the management of these changes in Scandinavia has been strongly influenced by the high profile of national and local governments in the provision of social services. There have, however, been considerable variations in policy between the three countries. Norway was enjoying a flow of oil wealth at a time when Denmark was experiencing severe balance-of-payments problems. Centre-right coalitions have governed Denmark and Norway for much of the 1970s and 1980s but the Social Democrats regained political control in Sweden, presiding over a run-down of declining manufacturing industries at the same time as centre-right governments were subsidizing the equivalent Norwegian industries. There have also been differences in transport and energy policy. The Swedes agreed to close down their nuclear power stations during the period when the Norwegians were actively developing North Sea oil. The Danes have built more transport infrastructure and allowed more competition in transport than their neighbours.

However, the 1990s promise to be a decade of convergence in industrial and energy policy, partly influenced by Nordic Council policies and partly by the prospect of closer integration within the EC. More energy is now flowing from the North Sea across Scandinavia. Transport policies that have appeared successful in one country have been modified and applied to the other two. At the same time, manufacturing firms are forging new links across national boundaries. Closer integration of the Norwegian and Swedish economies with Europe might well involve modifications to the 'social democratic consensus', which has prevailed in Scandinavia for much of the twentieth century. There are certain inflationary tendencies inherent in the Welfare State and its objective of equality of opportunity. Scandinavian firms would become more liable to take-over by foreign multinationals, while the agricultural and manufacturing industries would be increasingly conscious of their high labour costs relative to other EC producers.

FOUR

Urban Issues

4.1 Population change

Scandinavia's area is slightly larger than that of England and Wales, and Germany and Italy combined, but its population of 17.7 million is less than one tenth as large. Within Scandinavia there is a sharp contrast in density of settlement between Denmark's moderate 119 persons per km^2 and the very low densities of 13 per km^2 in Norway and 19 per km^2 in Sweden. They reflect the different resource bases, and especially the fact that three quarters of Norway, and one third of Sweden, is unproductive, either bare rock, above the tree line or waterlogged. Outside Denmark the population density only approaches the European average of 100 persons per km^2 in the southern Swedish province of Skåne, whilst large areas have densities under 1 person per km^2. Stone (1962, 1971) distinguishes between the 'continuous settlement zone', covering the whole of Denmark, most of Sweden south of 60°N and the Oslofjord, and south- and west-coast margins of Norway, and the 'fringe zones' of discontinuous linear settlement elsewhere, which follow the coastline and inland valleys.

4.1.1 Growth and redistribution of population

Scandinavia's population increased from 4.2 million in 1800 to 14.6 million in 1950, at a rate averaging 1 per cent per year. Denmark's and Norway's later fall in birth rate and Denmark's lower level of transatlantic emigration yielded considerably faster growth in Denmark and slightly faster growth in Norway than in Sweden. Population growth dipped in the 1950s in Denmark and Sweden and in the 1960s in Norway to a common +0.8 per cent per annum growth rate, which masked substantial regional differences.

The 1960s were a period of strong population growth, above the average 8 per cent, in all the metropolitan and large urban areas of Scandinavia, and also in west Jutland, south-west Norway and west coast Sweden, which all face the main European markets (Figures 4.1, 4.2 and

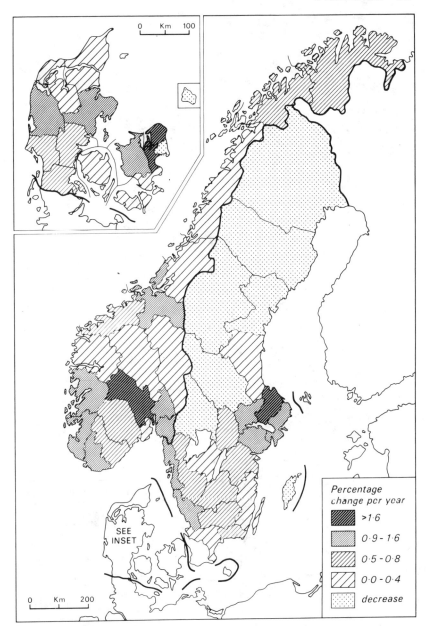

Figure 4.1 Population change, 1960–70 (Denmark, 1965–70)

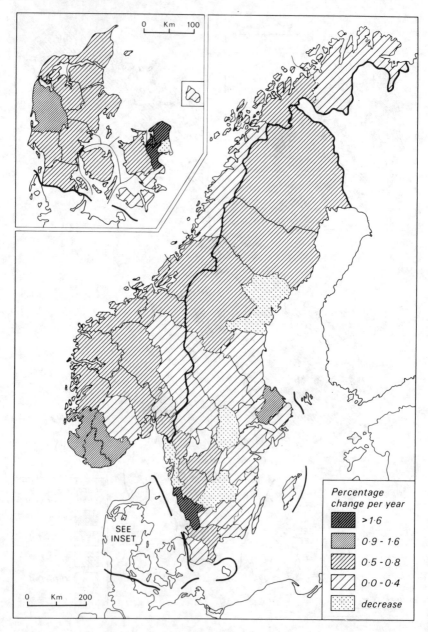

Figure 4.2 Population change, 1970–80

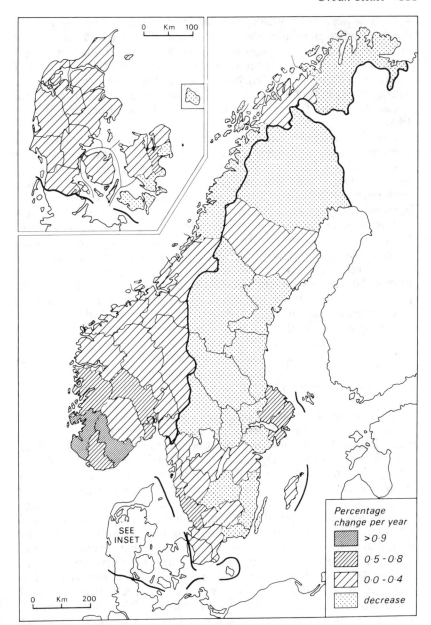

Figure 4.3 Population change, 1980–88

4.3). However, in Denmark, population loss occurred on the isolated Baltic island of Bornholm and in Storstrøms (Table 4.1). Every county in Norway increased in population, even in the north where the high birth rate more than offset the high net outmigration (Table 4.2). All of northern Sweden (except Gävleborg) lost population because of heavy net outmigration, as did the west Swedish midlands and the island of Gotland (Table 4.3). Jämtland in the northern interior lost 10 per cent (Illeris, 1990).

The 1970s marked a watershed in Scandinavian population development as growth rates halved due to a slump in birth rates to below replacement level, which was caused by the widespread use of contraception and abortion. Throughout Scandinavia internal migration subsided and low birth rates became universal, even in peripheral areas (Myklebost, 1976). Regional variations in population change also declined within Denmark and Sweden. Denmark's capital region lost population whilst the rest of Denmark increased its population, although only Århus grew strongly (Court, 1989). In Norway, Rogaland/Agder in the south west grew strongly because of North Sea oil and gas activity and proximity to Europe, both factors attracting inmigrants. A strong regional development policy sustained population growth in all of Norway's peripheral counties and dampened growth in the Oslofjord area in a period of much lower and more uniform birth rates. In Sweden only Uppsala and Halland grew strongly, as overspill areas for Stockholm and Gothenburg respectively. Seven counties declined, including three in the north Swedish midlands whose old industrial base was contracting. All of northern Sweden, except Västernorrland, grew with the aid of an effective regional development policy.

In the 1980s, Denmark's population stabilized, Sweden's grew by 0.1 per cent per year, whilst Norway's continued to grow at 0.3 per cent per year. Regional variations in population change again declined within Denmark and Sweden. Denmark's capital region continued to decline slowly whilst the 1960s pattern of population loss re-occurred in peripheral Bornholm and Storstrøms. The resumption of heavy outmigration from peripheral Norway, particularly to the Oslo area, boosted Greater Oslo's growth and caused population loss in north Norway and Hedmark (Hansen, 1989). Only Rogaland continued to grow strongly, although inmigration fell from 1985 after oil and gas activity passed its peak. West-coast Sweden and the three metropolitan areas have grown slowly in the 1980s but 12 of Sweden's 24 counties have lost population. This includes all of northern Sweden, except for Västerbotten, the north Swedish midlands and the south-east mainland. This was the third successive decade of population loss for peripheral Värmland and Västernorrland, whilst four other counties had also declined in the 1970s.

Table 4.1 Denmark: population change by counties, 1965–88

County	Population total				Population change per year (%)		
	1965	1970	1980	1988	1965–70	1970–80	1980–8
Stor København*	1,347,397	1,339,906	1,214,382	1,159,645	−0.1	−0.9	−0.6
Frederiksborg	211,449	259,439	329,141	339,914	+4.5	+2.7	+0.4
Roskilde	118,768	153,256	202,017	215,164	+5.8	+3.2	+0.8
Vestsjællands	248,391	259,089	277,833	282,775	+0.9	+0.7	+0.2
Storstrøms	252,498	252,370	260,081	257,161	−0.0	+0.3	−0.1
Bornholms	48,954	47,253	47,780	46,642	−0.7	+0.1	−0.3
Fyns	425,128	432,765	452,965	457,070	+0.4	+0.5	+0.1
Sønderjyllands	230,903	238,075	249,949	250,132	+0.6	+0.5	+0.0
Ribe	190,672	197,841	212,624	217,973	+0.8	+0.7	+0.3
Vejle	293,906	306,280	325,774	329,590	+0.8	+0.6	+0.1
Ringkøbing	231,002	241,352	262,751	266,554	+0.9	+0.9	+0.2
Århus	498,291	533,193	573,916	591,993	+1.4	+0.8	+0.4
Viborg	219,626	220,753	231,517	230,966	+0.1	+0.5	−0.0
Nordjyllands	450,822	456,212	481,335	483,675	+0.2	+0.6	+0.1
Denmark	4,767,597	4,937,784	5,122,065	5,129,254	+0.7	+0.4	+0.0

* Copenhagen City, Frederiksberg Town and Copenhagen County.
Source: *Statistisk Årbog Danmark* (1989).

Table 4.2 Norway: population change by counties, 1960–88

County	Population total				Population change per year (%)		
	1960	1970	1980	1988	1960–70	1970–80	1980–8
Østfold	202,751	221,386	233,301	237,045	+0.9	+0.5	+0.2
Akershus/Oslo	709,986	805,938	821,216	859,721	+1.4	+0.2	+0.6
Hedmark	177,324	179,204	187,223	186,418	+0.1	+0.4	−0.1
Oppland	166,303	172,479	180,765	182,341	+0.4	+0.5	+0.1
Buskerud	168,351	198,852	214,571	223,266	+1.8	+0.8	+0.5
Vestfold	174,382	175,402	186,691	194,477	+0.1	+0.6	+0.5
Telemark	149,943	156,778	162,050	163,240	+0.5	+0.3	+0.1
Aust-Agder	77,066	80,839	90,629	96,011	+0.5	+1.2	+0.7
Vest-Agder	109,083	124,171	136,718	142,015	+1.4	+1.0	+0.5
Rogaland	239,052	268,684	305,490	329,542	+1.2	+1.4	+1.0
Hordaland	341,303	373,843	391,463	405,063	+1.0	+0.5	+0.4
Sogn og Fjordane	99,957	100,933	105,924	106,066	+0.1	+0.5	+0.0
Møre og Romsdal	213,286	223,709	236,062	237,599	+0.5	+0.6	+0.1
Sør-Trøndelag	211,819	234,022	244,760	248,076	+1.0	+0.5	+0.2
Nord-Trøndelag	116,760	117,998	125,835	126,769	+0.1	+0.7	+0.1
Nordland	237,530	240,951	244,493	240,078	+0.1	+0.1	−0.2
Troms	127,771	136,805	146,818	146,489	+0.7	+0.7	−0.0
Finnmark	72,104	76,311	78,331	74,073	+0.6	+0.3	−0.7
Norway	3,594,771	3,888,305	4,092,340	4,198,289	+0.8	+0.5	+0.3

Source: *Statistisk Årbok Norway* (1988 and 1989).

Table 4.3 Sweden: population change by counties, 1960–88

County	Population total				Population change per year (%)		
	1960	1970	1980	1988	1960–70	1970–80	1980–8
Stockholms	1,271,014	1,478,015	1,518,200	1,606,157	+1.6	+0.3	+0.6
Uppsala	167,722	217,730	243,585	257,739	+3.0	+1.2	+0.7
Södermanlands	227,807	248,413	252,536	250,073	+0.9	+0.2	−0.1
Östergötlands	357,601	382,675	392,789	395,580	+0.7	+0.3	+0.1
Jönköpings	285,348	306,649	303,156	302,475	+0.7	−0.1	−0.0
Kronobergs	158,867	166,736	173,691	174,116	+0.5	+0.4	+0.0
Kalmar	235,612	241,026	241,581	237,356	+0.2	+0.0	−0.2
Gotlands	54,196	53,723	55,346	56,269	−0.1	+0.3	+0.2
Blekinge	144,466	153,585	153,542	149,600	+0.6	−0.0	−0.3
Kristianstads	256,395	264,170	280,193	281,907	+0.3	+0.6	+0.1
Malmöhus	626,086	719,599	743,286	757,643	+1.5	+0.3	+0.2
Hallands	169,995	193,108	230,924	244,377	+1.4	+2.0	+0.7
Göteborgs och Bohus	625,670	715,289	711,195	726,325	+1.4	−0.1	+0.3
Älvsborgs	374,683	403,711	425,452	430,129	+0.8	+0.5	+0.1
Skaraborgs	249,948	257,301	269,730	270,847	+0.3	+0.5	+0.1
Värmlands	291,074	284,688	284,070	279,402	−0.2	−0.0	−0.2
Örebro	262,321	276,799	274,356	269,431	+0.6	−0.1	−0.2
Västmanlands	232,973	260,293	259,538	254,253	+1.3	−0.0	−0.3
Kopparbergs	286,047	277,058	286,968	283,330	−0.3	+0.4	−0.2
Gävleborgs	293,246	293,459	294,020	286,907	+0.0	+0.0	−0.3
Västernorrlands	285,676	273,456	267,935	260,332	−0.4	−0.2	−0.4
Jämtlands	139,799	125,243	134,934	133,389	−1.0	+0.8	−0.1
Västerbottens	239,619	233,134	243,856	245,703	−0.3	+0.5	+0.1
Norrbottens	261,802	255,369	267,054	260,833	−0.2	+0.5	−0.3
Sweden	7,497,967	8,081,229	8,317,937	8,414,083	+0.8	+0.3	+0.1

Source: *Statistisk Årsbok Sweden* (1988 and 1990).

As both birth rates and the rate of population growth declined in the 1960s, immigration of foreign workers became important for the first time in modern Scandinavia. Intra-Nordic immigration has increased due to post-war co-operation leading to a free labour market. However, the only substantial intra-Nordic movement is of Finns, many with Swedish as their first language, to the more prosperous Swedish economy. The current total of 131,000 Finns resident in Sweden is only one third of the 1970 peak figure of 400,000 and reflects the growth in Finnish living standards since 1970. The rapid growth of southern European and Asian immigration was more significant from the mid-1960s to the 1970s, filling gaps in the Scandinavian labour markets. Immigration of workers from non-Nordic countries has virtually ceased since the mid-1970s economic downturn and secondary immigration of family members has gradually reduced (Swedish Institute, 1989c). Scandinavia has also acted as a significant haven for political refugees from the Middle East, the Baltic states, Chile and Vietnam. Non-Nordic residents now account for 2.5 per cent of the Swedish population and more than 2 per cent of both the Danish and Norwegian populations (Table 4.4). The largest non-EC/ EFTA ethnic minority groups are Yugoslavs in Sweden, Turks in Denmark and Sweden, Iranians in Sweden and Pakistanis in Norway.

4.1.2 Urbanization

Scandinavia is now a highly urbanized area, with 84 per cent of Danes, 71 per cent of Norwegians and 83 per cent of Swedes living in *tettsteder* (urban places of at least 200 people) in 1980−1 (Table 4.5; Myklebost, 1960). Even using the international urban threshold of 20,000 people, 50

Table 4.4 Population by citizenship, 1988

	Denmark	Norway	Sweden
Total population	5,129,254	4,198,289	8,414,083
Nordic	23,130	35,676	186,290
	(0.45%)	(0.85%)	(2.21%)
Non-Nordic*	113,047	87,999	214,684
	(2.2%)	(2.1%)	(2.55%)

* Main non-Nordic groups: *Denmark* − Turkey, 24,423; UK, 10,096; other Asian, 10,036; *Norway* − UK, 12,770; Pakistan, 10,252; USA, 10,099; *Sweden* − Yugoslavia, 38,723; Turkey, 22,414; Iran, 20,463.
Source: *Yearbook of Nordic Statistics* (1988).

Table 4.5 Scandinavian urban population by settlement size, 1980−1

Settlement size	Denmark (1981)		Norway (1980)		Sweden (1980)	
	Population	%	Population	%	Population	%
200−499	198,077	3.9	107,298	2.6	221,730	2.7
500−999	237,755	4.6	143,413	3.5	295,702	3.6
1,000−1,999	301,885	5.9	191,309	4.7	384,523	4.6
2,000−9,999	719,829	14.0	588,756	14.4	1,410,273	16.9
10,000−19,999	296,549	5.8	201,886	4.9	887,445	10.7
20,000−49,999	601,385	11.7	439,775	10.7	976,904	11.7
50,000+	1,941,612	37.9	1,209,828	29.6	2,736,916	32.9
Total urban	4,297,092	83.9	2,882,265	70.5	6,913,493	83.1
Total population	5,123,989	100.0	4,091,132	100.0	8,320,438	100.0

Source: *Yearbook of Nordic Statistics* (1988).

per cent of Danes, 40 per cent of Norwegians and 45 per cent of Swedes are urban dwellers. Small towns offer a surprisingly high level of services to wide areas, and have become increasingly attractive to migrants as a post-industrial society develops. In each country over a quarter of the total population live in towns of under 10,000 people.

Scandinavia's urban majorities are, however, of relatively recent origin as industrialization and associated urbanization were delayed by the virtual absence of indigenous coal supplies. Norway only became a mainly urban country as recently as 1946, fifteen years after Sweden and 36 years later than Denmark − historically the most urbanized country in Scandinavia.

Most of the 84 Danish towns existing in 1900 were coastal towns created by royal charter, mainly in the Middle Ages. Their trade monopolies survived until 1857, whilst some commerce and trades privileges were not abolished until 1931, thus restricting the emergence of new towns and hindering the development of a normal settlement hierarchy (Kampp, 1987). The major exception was the new town and port of Esbjerg, established in 1868 to export agricultural produce from the heathlands of Jutland, newly colonized in response to the loss of Slesvig-Holstein to Prussia in 1864.

Copenhagen dominates Danish urban settlement because of its key trading position at the mouth of the Baltic Sea, and because of its function (from 1416) as the capital of Denmark. Copenhagen's population grew strongly from 130,000 in 1850, to 454,000 in 1901, due to steady industrial growth, its magnetic attraction for most rural migrants, to the lifting of building restrictions outside the medieval ramparts in 1852 and 1867 and to boundary extensions. After 1901, Copenhagen's primacy within Denmark was further enhanced by the rapid growth of suburbs and dormitory towns.

In the 1960s, growth slowed as the pool of surplus rural dwellers dried up and, by 1974, ceased when the population reached 1.4 million in Greater Copenhagen and 1.75 million in the Copenhagen Metropolitan Region. Copenhagen City had already experienced a sharp decline in its 1950 peak population of 768,000 as a result of smaller families, urban renewal at lower densities and static city boundaries; in the 1980s its population fell below 500,000 and stabilized. The slight decline in the population of Greater Copenhagen and the Metropolitan Region in the 1970s and 1980s was identified as desurbanization by Matthiessen (1980). Desurbanization occurs when either net inmigration is exceeded by a surplus of deaths over births, or where net outmigration exceeds a surplus of births over deaths, or accompanies a surplus of deaths as the birth rate dips below replacement level. In the 1970s and 1980s the centuries-old pattern of net inmigration to Copenhagen reversed as smaller towns became more attractive places in which to live and work in an increasingly post-industrial society. At the same time, Copenhagen's birth rate declined to well below replacement level.

In contrast to Copenhagen, the larger provincial towns of Århus, Odense, Ålborg and Esbjerg were aided by an active regional development policy and continued to grow and suburbanize, albeit less strongly after 1970. Smaller towns are now growing most strongly.

Two types of urban settlement existed in pre-industrial Norway. *Bysteder* (towns or cities) were usually located on the coast and were established by charter, with areas of trade monopoly, which, in Bergen's case, covered the whole of west and north Norway. Ten *bysteder* existed before 1580, seven of them in south-east Norway, whilst Bergen, Stavanger and Trondheim stood out as isolated urban settlements. In 1900 there were forty *bysteder*, of which only four were in north Norway. Until 1953, *bysteder* were given separate representation to rural areas in the Norwegian parliament. *Kjøpsteder* (market towns), however, had no privileges beyond their role as local market-places and were consequently much smaller. Oslo (called Kristiania until 1925) grew rapidly as Norway's capital and main port, especially after the development of railways and the onset of industrialization. In spite of a major boundary extension to the city in 1948, most of the subsequent population increase has occurred in suburbs outside the city, but Greater Oslo's primacy in Norway remains unchallenged. The city's population peaked at 470,000 in 1960 and has since declined to 450,000.

Myklebost (1984) highlights the vigorous expansion of many small centres in Norway with populations ranging from 5,000 to as small as 300, filling the gap caused by the absence of a village tradition. The late development of cities in many regions resulted in a weakly developed regional settlement hierarchy; consequently most rural migrants were attracted to Oslo and, to a lesser, extent Bergen. From the 1960s new regional centres, such as Tromsø, Bodø and Kongsvinger, emerged, with the support of regional development policies, as countermagnets for local migrants. North Sea oil and gas development in the 1970s boosted the growth of Stavanger and Sandnes in south-west Norway.

In Sweden medieval towns were established mainly in the central belt from Stockholm and Uppsala in the east, to Gothenburg in the west, and in the then Danish-controlled southern areas of Halland and Skåne. None of the 50 settlements granted town status before 1580 were in the north. By 1900 a further 42 towns were established. Sweden's larger size and resource base, and the Baltic-coast location of its capital, Stockholm, remote from European markets, gave room for Gothenburg and Malmö to grow as independent centres on Sweden's short western coast.

From the 1920s to the 1960s massive migration from rural areas fuelled the growth of Stockholm and, to a lesser extent, Gothenburg and Malmö. From the 1950s suburban growth dominated. The population of the central cities declined in Stockholm after 1960 and in Gothenburg and Malmö after 1970, as a result of smaller families, inner-area redevelopment at lower densities and the reaction against living in apartments in anonymous, concrete, tower blocks. Growing affluence and car ownership and tax-deductible mortgage interest and commuting costs have all encouraged the growth of villages and small towns within the three metropolitan areas and beyond.

The rapid growth of middle-sized towns was encouraged from the 1950s by government regional development policy, including the decentralization of government offices and agency headquarters to provincial towns, and the policy of developing higher education in county towns, while local-government reform greatly encouraged the growth of municipality centres.

4.2 Housing

A social-democratic consensus of equal access for all regardless of social class, to suitable modern, well-equipped and affordable housing has been accepted in Sweden since the 1930s and Denmark and Norway since 1945. The vast majority of dwellings in all three countries are of post-war construction and there is now no longer a housing shortage in Scandinavia as there was throughout the period of rapid urbanization up to the 1970s.

The huge increase in the number of dwellings since 1945, a doubling in Norway's case, reflects an increased population, an even faster rise in the number of households with many more single-person households and fewer children and also less overcrowding. Although over 90 per cent of rural dwellings in all three countries are owner-occupied family houses, there are substantial differences in urban housing types and ownership. Two thirds of urban dwellers in Norway are owner-occupiers mainly in family houses compared with a slim majority in Denmark. In contrast, two thirds live in rented apartments or group accommodation in Sweden (Table 4.6). However, there are common urban trends in all three countries away from building apartment blocks for rent towards more owner-occupied, mainly detached, family housing. Some emphasis has also been placed on the renovation and upgrading rather than demolition of tenements and apartment blocks in the older, inner suburbs. With an ageing population, more dwellings have been constructed for elderly persons.

4.2.1   Sweden

As a reaction to private rented housing and social segregation, suburbs of mainly publicly rented apartment blocks were developed for a mixture of social classes from the 1930s onwards, but particularly from the 1950s, in Stockholm, Gothenburg, Malmö and medium-sized Swedish towns. Three- to four-storey blocks lost favour in the 1950s to seven- to eight-storey blocks and to even higher tower blocks in the 1960s built in near-uniform suburbs. From the 1960s many apartments were larger and better equipped with four rooms plus a kitchen. Between 1965 and 1974 the ten-year programme to build almost a million high-standard apartments in blocks finally overcame Sweden's long-standing housing shortage (Table 4.6). Special means-tested housing subsidies offset the high rents for lower-income households. Although these planned suburbs with their well-equipped apartments were pedestrianized and had good services with shops, schools, day nurseries, public transport and sports facilities within walking distance, they were increasingly criticized as dull, bleak and soulless.

Since the mid-1970s the Swedish urban housing market has altered significantly. A combination of the much lower birth rates and an ending of traditional rural-labour shedding and consequent rural-to-urban migration led to a new and unforeseen surplus of unlet apartments. This introduced unintentional choice into the urban housing market at a time when unsurpassed prosperity enabled most Swedish families to buy cars and allowed social segregation to occur on a large scale for the first time since the Social Democrats took power in the mid-1930s. After 1974 total

Table 4.6 Urban and rural housing types

		Urban			Rural			Total		
		Family houses	Other*		Family houses	Other*		Family houses	Other*	
		No. %	No. %		No. %	No. %		No. %	No. %	
Denmark	1960	390,690 37.6	647,130 62.4		428,050 96.2	17,030 3.8		818,740 55.2	664,160 44.8	
	1970	704,044 47.1	789,524 52.9		300,807 98.0	6,279 2.0		1,004,851 55.8	795,803 44.2	
	1989	1,030,530 52.5	931,755 47.5		333,655 91.2	32,353 8.8		1,364,185 58.6	964,108 41.4	
Norway	1960	144,341 37.1	244,954 62.9		596,131 86.9	89,719 13.1		740,472 68.9	334,673 31.1	
	1970	460,673 51.8	429,428 48.2		377,720 92.9	28,939 7.1		838,393 64.7	458,367 35.3	
	1980	684,847 66.5	345,232 33.5		355,570 96.0	14,766 4.0		1,040,417 74.3	359,998 25.7	
Sweden	1960	632,451 31.6	1,366,246 68.4		625,604 92.5	50,794 7.5		1,258,055 47.0	1,417,040 53.0	
	1970	822,715 31.2	1,812,627 68.8		514,886 94.3	31,011 5.7		1,337,601 42.0	1,843,638 58.0	
	1985	n.a.	n.a.		n.a.	n.a.		1,778,128 46.0	2,085,311 54.0	

n.a. – not available.
* Mainly apartment blocks and some group accommodation for the elderly and disabled.
Source: *Yearbook of Nordic Statistics* (1989–90).

housing construction was drastically reduced and three quarters of all new dwellings constructed were private family houses. This revealed latent demands for home ownership and for more spacious housing, which had been suppressed for forty years, and a rejection of publicly rented high-rise apartments without defensible space by families who could afford to move. To overcome the loss of rent from unlet apartments, the housing corporations were forced to accept anyone who wished to be a tenant, including many young single adults, the growing number of single and divorced mothers and people with social problems who previously had been unable to obtain housing easily. Between 1970 and 1985 single-person households increased from 25.3 per cent to 36.1 per cent of the total, whilst households with three or more persons declined from 45.2 per cent to 32.5 per cent. Foreign immigrants and refugees from Yugoslavia, Turkey, Iran, South America and, to a lesser degree, Finland, added a new and sometimes unwanted diversity of culture to high-rise suburbs, which provoked a racialist backlash from a minority of Swedes. A higher incidence of unemployment, vandalism, alcoholism, drug abuse, school drop-out and low-income population became a feature of the increasingly segregated publicly rented apartments (Daun, 1985). In contrast, the tenant-owned and managed co-operative housing-association apartment blocks remained popular with Swedish families because of lower tenant turnover and greater control over the environment, public space, vandalism and lettings.

Since the mid-1970s the very basis of Sweden's Social-Democratic Welfare State has been increasingly questioned. From 1976 to 1982 a weak centre and right government temporarily interrupted Social Democratic rule in Sweden without radically changing Swedish society. In the 1980s new urban housing development has been dominated by private, mainly detached family houses, usually located away from the planned suburbs. New apartments are now more attractively and personally designed, most are owned and managed by tenant housing associations and built by the large Riksbyggen and HSB housing corporations. Independent private housing-association developments are built by smaller building companies. However, the rents for new apartments have increased faster than housing subsidies, making them too expensive for many people. In the deteriorating municipally owned apartments, attempts at tenant involvement in management have met with little success.

Although the number of rural dwellings has fallen in Sweden, and many have been converted to second homes, the quality of rural housing facilities has been transformed to add to their greater spaciousness and more desirable location. Whereas in 1960 only 49 per cent of rural dwellings had central heating, 37 per cent a WC and 28 per cent a bathroom, compared with 82 per cent, 81 per cent and 62 per cent in urban dwellings, by 1985 nearly all urban and rural dwellings in Sweden had all three facilities.

4.2.2 Denmark

Although the majority of Danish dwellings are private family houses, this was only achieved in urban areas in the 1980s despite incentives such as tax relief on mortgage interest, house maintenance and property taxes (Table 4.6). Mortgages in Denmark are administered by special mortgage societies with top-up loans from central and local government.

Prior to the 1980s, apartments formed the majority of urban dwellings. There is a long history of apartment dwelling in Copenhagen dating back to the many one- and two-room dwellings in cramped five-storey buildings within the defensive ramparts. Until 1852 the ramparts marked the limit of urban development with 130,000 people living in a 3-km^2 area. This tradition was continued after 1852 by the intensive private development of five- and six-storey tenement blocks on a grid-iron street pattern in the bridge quarters beyond the ramparts, where 180,000 people lived by 1900. Housing co-operatives started with the Burmeister shipyard workers in 1865, developed as non-profit-making associations from 1912 but only started on a large scale when State building subsidies were introduced in 1938. These subsidies replaced the 1887 policy of loans to build low-rent housing. By 1973 Denmark had 650 housing associations, some of them co-operatives, some housing companies and other self-governing associations, but all with tenant management and about half with local-authority involvement (Ministry of Housing, 1974). Unlike Sweden, direct State or local-government ownership of housing is an insignificant 2 per cent, mainly consisting of dwellings for public employees and, in large cities, dwellings for the elderly and disabled.

Over half the dwellings built in Denmark in the 1920s and 1930s were apartments, mainly in Copenhagen, which was growing rapidly. Rent controls since 1945 and direct means-tested subsidies to occupiers of rented dwellings encouraged further apartment development. Local and national government also supported housing for pensioners and the disabled, which was integrated into the wider community. From 1947 rapid urban expansion was concentrated in Copenhagen in apartment development around stations in the five radial rail corridors of the 1947 Finger Plan. The 1963 First Step Plan extended this type of development further along the corridors towards Roskilde and Køge. By 1973 Denmark's, and particularly Copenhagen's, housing shortage was over as a much reduced birth rate and a reversal of rural-to-urban migration halted urban population growth. From 1974, apartment building more than halved from nearly 18,000 a year, and social segregation increased as more Danes chose to buy new detached housing, often in locations made more accessible by car. Two thirds of new family houses had four rooms or more, with an average 140 m^2 of space compared with an average 80 m^2 in apartments. Housing associations started to develop more low-rise terraced and cluster houses.

The proportion of one-person households jumped from 23.7 per cent in 1970 to 33.1 per cent in 1989, whereas three or more person households declined from 46.8 per cent to 34.1 per cent. Denmark has retained over half-a-million pre-1920 dwellings, many more than either Norway or Sweden. The Preservation of Buildings Act 1918 was an early Danish initiative, whilst the Slum Clearance Act 1969, despite its name, provides subsidies and loans for renovating, converting and improving old buildings, especially tenement blocks in Copenhagen's bridge quarters. In the less attractive Køge Bay finger suburbs, apartments became hard to let because rents were high compared with the inner city, and transport links were poor as electric-railway construction from Copenhagen lagged behind urban development until 1983. Foreign immigrants gravitated to finger suburbs such as Ishøj and to unimproved inner-area nineteenth-century tenements. In 1982 seven suburban municipalities were restricting immigration on the basis of income, whilst two of them, Ishøj and Høje Tåstrup, specifically limited ethnic minorities to a maximum of 10 per cent of the total population. In the last 30 years the quality of Danish urban and rural housing facilities has been transformed. In 1960 only 27 per cent of rural dwellings and 56 per cent of urban dwellings had central heating, 54 per cent and 96 per cent respectively had a WC and 30 per cent and 56 per cent respectively a bathroom. By 1989, the rural/urban differences had been eliminated, with central heating in 94 per cent of all dwellings, a WC in 96 per cent and a bathroom in 88 per cent. In the late 1980s reduced tax relief for home-owners and other austerity measures have encouraged a shift back from owning to renting apartments.

4.2.3 Norway

Norway's high proportion of owner-occupied family houses is largely the result of the Social Democratic policy of home-ownership (Table 4.6). Rasmussen (1985, p. 292) explains that, in the 1950s, 'the Labour Party was the party of those who lived in rented houses and it championed the idea that no one should profit from the housing needs of others', whilst the Conservative Party was supported by private landlords who rented out dwellings. Now Conservatives defend house-owners against high tax assessments.

In the 1980s the State Housing Bank provided about 55 per cent of home buyers with low-start, low-cost loans and the State Agricultural

Bank provided for a further 5 per cent situated on agricultural holdings. Together they have funded three quarters of home buyers since 1945; top-up loans are provided by private credit institutions. Tax relief on mortgage interest has also assisted home buyers. Norway's massive housing shortage was not overcome until 1981 because, unlike Sweden and Denmark, Norway had, first, to replace housing destroyed during the Second World War by the retreating German army in 1945, throughout Finnmark county and the eastern half of Troms county, and in fire-bombed towns such as Bodø and Molde. Second, Norway had to make up for the lack of house building during the occupation. Norway's urbanization process and birth-rate decline were also later and slower. During the 1950s and 1960s, nearly 30,000 dwellings a year were built, increasing to 39,000 per year in the 1970s. As the housing shortage disappeared, dwelling construction dropped back to 30,000 in 1984. During the period from 1951 to 1980, three quarters of new dwellings in Norway were detached or semi-detached family houses, and only 25 per cent apartment blocks or group housing compared with 70 per cent in Sweden.

Norway's post-war urban development has, therefore, been low density and very spread out because family housing has been encouraged by fiercely independent suburban and rural municipalities beyond the already developed central cities, and house building has normally been prohibited on arable land since the Agriculture Act 1955. By the 1980s most active urban development was 40−60 km from Oslo and 20−30 km from the core of other large Norwegian cities. Ownership of a high-quality and spacious detached house outweighs the cost and time of long-distance commuting by car, bus and, in Oslo's case, rail. Norway's 454 municipalities are the housing authorities and in 1981, 60 per cent of them had housing programmes, purchasing land and developing infrastructure with loans from the State Municipal Bank, so that small private developers can construct new houses. Municipalities also process home-buyers' loans from the State Housing Bank. Norway's broad political consensus on housing policy and strong government involvement has ensured a consistent programme of house building without the marked fluctuations experienced, for example, in Britain (Ministry of Local Government and Labour, 1982). However, as in Denmark, State and municipal ownership of housing is of little importance in Norway, totalling only 5 per cent of all dwellings − mainly rented dwellings for pensioners and some very poor families in great need.

Despite the heavy dominance of home-ownership in Norway as a whole, most urban dwellings were rented apartments or group accommodation until the late 1960s. Norway's first co-operative housing society was OBOS (Oslo Housing and Savings Society) established in 1929, which

Oslo city supported instead of producing its own housing (Pooley, 1989). After 1945, co-operative and other non-profit housing greatly expanded, developing most of Norway's apartment blocks, especially in the satellite suburbs to the east and south of Oslo. Social segregation has grown between the richer west and poorer east and south of Oslo. In large urban areas, as land prices are too high for new detached family houses, the State Housing Bank usually only lends on apartment blocks and terraced houses. As a result, Oslo and Akershus had 34 per cent co-operatively owned dwellings and private share-owners by 1981, twice the national average. They also had 20-per-cent ordinary tenants, half as much again as in the rest of Norway. The ending of Norway's housing shortage led to unlet apartments in some parts of Oslo from 1980. Rent control since 1967 has kept down housing costs on private and co-operatively rented dwellings in over 100 urban and suburban municipalities. A means-tested housing subsidy to 100,000 low-income households cover 65 per cent of the difference, 80 per cent in the case of pensioners and the disabled, between the cost of housing and an assumed reasonable household expenditure on housing. Housing for Norway's 80,000 immigrants is helped by SIBO, the Immigrant Housing Co-operative, with 1,000 dwellings, mainly older apartment blocks in inner Oslo. The FLYBO foundation builds and administers housing for some of the 10,000 refugees resident in Norway. Special housing is also provided for drug- and alcohol-addicted young people, for single pregnant women, the disabled and vagrants.

In the 1970s the share of new apartment blocks halved to 11 per cent of all dwellings, while semi-detached and terraced housing nearly doubled to 38 per cent. Renovation of older housing became an alternative to slum clearance with means-tested, low-cost, low-start improvement loans and grants. Some 2,000 dwellings a year were improved in inner Oslo, half of them through the partly municipally owned Oslo Urban Renewal Ltd, and a further 500 dwellings a year in Trondheim (Ministry of Local Government and Labour, 1982). Parts of run-down Grønlandtorget in inner-east Oslo have become gentrified by young, childless, professional people.

The proportion of single-person households in Norway rose from 21.1 per cent in 1970 to 27.9 per cent in 1980 but, unlike Denmark and Sweden, the only households to decline significantly were those with five or more persons from 16.9 per cent to 12.0 per cent as Norway's birth rate declined more slowly.

The number of rural dwellings in Norway has declined, with a particularly sharp fall in the 1960s, although some have been converted to second homes. Although Norway's rural dwellings are more spacious and their facilities have improved, they are still less well equipped than

Norway's urban dwellings. In 1960 a mere 36 per cent of rural dwellings and 61 per cent of urban dwellings had a bathroom whilst 33 per cent and 66 per cent respectively had a WC. By 1980 bathrooms were in 76 per cent of rural dwellings and 84 per cent of urban dwellings, whilst 74 per cent and 86 per cent respectively had a WC. All Norway's rural and urban dwellings are connected to its very cheap hydro-electricity supply, which is used to heat most Norwegian homes so that centrally controlled heating systems are not common.

4.2.4 Second homes

A distinctive aspect of Scandinavian housing is the very large number of second homes, particularly in Sweden, with 625,000 in 1986, equivalent to 16 per cent of the permanent dwelling stock. In comparison, Norway had 170,000 second homes in 1971, equivalent to 13 per cent of its permanent dwelling stock and growing by 10,000 per year, whereas Denmark had 145,000 second homes in 1969, equivalent to 8 per cent of its permanent dwelling stock (Bielckus, 1977).

Second homes first developed in the early 1900s in the form of summer houses or *hagekoloni*, literally garden colonies, located mainly near to the large cities of Stockholm, Gothenburg, Copenhagen and Oslo. They provided open space for inner-area tenement and apartment dwellers and sometimes allotment gardening. Since the 1950s growing affluence has enabled many more second homes to be built or converted from agricultural use near the main towns and along the coasts. Mass car-ownership, improved roads, longer holidays and a shorter working week have encouraged more recent development in accessible mountain areas such as south Norrland and the Southern Uplands in Sweden and in southern Norway.

In Sweden, weekend and summer migrations to a holiday cottage are seen as the modern counterpart of farmers moving annually to summer pastures with their animals. In 1969 two thirds of Swedish second homes were owned by urban apartment dwellers. The release from agriculture of 10,000 rural family houses per year in the 1960s provided plenty of scope for new second homes. In the 1960s, 85 per cent of second homes were in central and southern Sweden and one third were within 20 km of urban areas with over 25,000 people. The coastal zone was most popular, especially in the west-coast areas of Bohuslän and Halland and in the Stockholm archipelago. The conversion of second homes into permanent dwellings is common in Sweden despite their often inadequate sewerage, poor water supplies and roads (Lewan, 1987). Almost half of second homes in Sweden are used as permanent summer residences. The 1966 Stockholm Regional Plan prohibited new development of holiday cottages within one hour's drive of the city centre to counter this conversion trend and to provide open space for daily recreation from the urban area. From the 1970s, greater planning controls prohibited new second homes above the tree line and rarely allowed their development within 300 m of the coast. Thousands of well-equipped caravan and camping sites have, in recent years, provided an alternative way to enjoy the countryside.

Denmark is a much more compact country with second-home development almost entirely coastal and purpose built. More than half are on the island of Sjælland where the huge demand from Copenhagen has been concentrated on the north coast, designated as a recreation area, and in Vestsjællands county. Since the 1960s thousands of summer cottages have been built in woodland away from permanent settlements. Some 80–90 per cent of Danish second homes lie within 60 km of their owner's first homes, although distances are increasing as sites become scarcer. The tendency towards permanent year-round occupation of second homes has been controlled by cutting off electricity supplies in winter to protect these environmentally attractive areas. Zoning laws prevent non-agricultural housing development in rural zones and urban development in summer-cottage zones.

In southern Norway, summer huts or cottages are very popular either to own or to rent. The highest demand is for converted, previously disused *seter* or mountain-pasture buildings, but there are many cottages on the coast, by lakes and in the forests. A very dispersed pattern has resulted from previous encouragement to farmers to build tourist huts to generate additional income. A new law in 1957 banned new huts from the shores and riversides of common land as common access had been increasingly denied. Summer cottages and huts provide an escape from 'urban uniformity and monotonous civilised comforts' according to Sund (1960, p. 287), and they keep Norwegians in touch with their rural roots.

The right of Scandinavians to buy farms owned by close relatives has enabled many urban dwellers to acquire second homes in rural areas from within their extended family. In Norway 90 per cent of farm-ownership changes are between close relatives. Long-distance and weekend commuting are also common as rural dwellings are cheaper and more spacious and are located in a better environment than many urban dwellings.

4.3   Land use and transport planning

As in cities the world over, Scandinavian planners have had to cope since 1945 with a rapid urbanization in order to accommodate large numbers of rural migrants and people displaced by the slum clearance of inner-area tenements, the natural growth of the existing urban population and also foreign immigrants and refugees. Urban growth began to slow down during the 1970s but marked changes in urban densities have continued to pose problems. City centres have increasingly been occupied by offices and public buildings; their population has been falling and becoming more elderly. The establishment of new households led to the rapid growth of suburbs, while the spread of car ownership resulted in the expansion of urban life-styles further and further into the surrounding countryside. It has been difficult to find room for all the suburban cars when they visit town centres, so the most celebrated shopping streets have been pedestrianized.

Scandinavian planners have had powerful weapons of intervention and control to channel these trends and a clear political agenda reflecting the overall welfare consensus of the Scandinavian peoples. The results contrast with the more market-oriented development and reactive urban planning in Britain and North America. Above all, Scandinavian planners have preserved the historical and cultural characters of old city centres, which have not been allowed to develop into mere central business districts. The characteristic groupings of skyscraper office blocks at the centres of North American cities have been shunned. Seen from out on the water, or from any eminence or tower, the historic spires and towers of Copenhagen, Oslo and Stockholm still maintain their unique skylines.

It is difficult to create equality of opportunity in the housing stock of a big city, but the worst housing inherited from the nineteenth century has been cleared away and the partnership between city governments, national housing banks and co-operative housing associations since the 1930s has produced a substantial amount of reasonable housing at affordable loans and rents. The large-scale acquisition of land by municipalities since the beginning of this century, including extensive areas surrounding the cities of Oslo and Stockholm, has facilitated the overall planning of land use and transport. The three Scandinavian capitals were pioneers in the creation of satellite towns with substantial local economies linked by electrified rapid-transit rail services to their city centres. They were among the first European capitals to implement master plans covering their whole metropolitan areas. As the sphere of metropolitan influence has widened, regional planning councils have been created.

So much is common to the major Scandinavian cities. The following examples illustrate how far the very different geographies of these conurbations have affected the plans made for them, and they also demonstrate some of the planning problems that have been encountered.

4.3.1 Copenhagen

The Copenhagen Metropolitan Region is Scandinavia's largest urban area with a 1989 population of 1.71 million, slightly below its 1975 peak of

1.77 million (Figure 4.4; Table 4.7). Since 1950 the population of the central cities of Copenhagen (Denmark's capital) and Frederiksberg have declined by 334,000 or 38 per cent, whilst neighbouring Copenhagen county almost doubled its 1950 population of 314,000 by 1980, although it has since slightly declined. Frederiksborg and Roskilde counties have grown continuously since 1950 from 238,000 to 557,000 in 1988, with the most rapid growth in the 1960s and 1970s and slower growth in the 1980s. The Metropolitan Region's growth of 273,000 or 19 per cent since 1950 has therefore been exceeded by internal relocation of population.

There is a long history of intervention and control in Copenhagen's development. By 1901 Copenhagen's population was 361,000; it was short of development land and was losing richer people to low-tax suburbs. Copenhagen's 1901 boundary extension trebled its area but failed to include the wealthy areas of Gentofte (14,000) and Frederiksberg (76,000), the latter becoming an enclave surrounded by Copenhagen. Copenhagen's new land was developed on a planned basis from 1909 as residential neighbourhoods were linked to the city centre by electrified trams, which were city owned from 1911 with a uniform fare to eliminate the cost of distance (Jensen, 1984).

After the German occupation, planners from the Danish Town Planning Institute formulated the advisory 1947 Finger Plan, as Copenhagen city was short of building land and was unable to obtain further boundary extensions. This co-ordinated the town planning of 29 municipalities and provided the framework for Greater Copenhagen's population growth to 1.4 million in 1965 and 1.7 million by 2000. The Finger Plan proposed five corridors or fingers of future urban development, mainly in Copenhagen county, along electrified S-train lines, with a new high-density suburb around each station like beads on a string. Following the 1936 Green Area Plan, green wedges of recreational and agricultural land were to be retained between each finger. Each station was expected to attract shopping development, whilst new subcentres at the base of each finger would be linked together by a ring road providing good decentralized locations for industry. These fingers of development are in marked contrast to the more concentric urban-development patterns of both the free-market and the green-belt-encircled city (City of Copenhagen, 1973; Figure 4.4). The Finger Plan deliberately avoided the coastal route to Helsingør to discourage further urban development along Denmark's riviera coast.

The Built-Up Area Regulation Act 1949, which required the zoning of urban development in large urban areas, was used by Copenhagen to activate the principles of the Finger Plan. However, in the 1950s Greater Copenhagen's population increased far more rapidly than anticipated. Unforeseen increases in private car-ownership also made many people independent of public transport and districts of lower-density detached

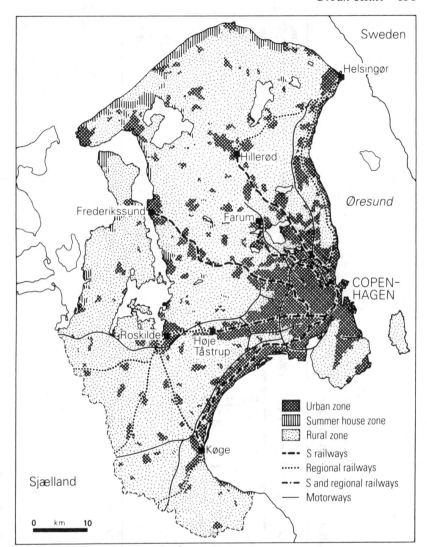

Figure 4.4 Copenhagen

houses flourished. The green wedges came under development pressure as the 1949 Act did not forbid the urbanization of agricultural land nor ensure co-operation between municipalities on a regional level. S-train development also did not always keep up with housing development.

Table 4.7 Copenhagen's population change, 1950–89 (000s)

	1950	1960	1970	1980	1989	% change 1950–70	% change 1970–89	% change 1950–89
1. Copenhagen city	768	721	623	499	468	−18.9	−24.9	−39.1
2. Frederiksberg	119	114	102	88	85	−14.4	−16.6	−28.6
3. Copenhagen county	314	486	615	627	602	+95.9	−2.1	+91.8
4. Greater Copenhagen (1, 2 and 3)	1,201	1,322	1,440	1,214	1,155	+19.9	−19.8	−3.8
5. Frederiksborg county	148	182	259	329	341	+75.0	+31.7	+130.4
6. Roskilde county	90	104	153	202	216	+70.0	+41.2	+140.0
7. Copenhagen Metropolitan Region (1, 2, 3, 5 and 6)	1,439	1,608	1,752	1,745	1,712	+21.8	−2.2	+19.0
8. Rest of Denmark	2,842	2,978	3,185	3,377	3,418	+12.1	+7.3	+20.3

Sources: *Københavns Statistiske Årbog* (1987); *Statistisk Årbog Danmark* (1989).

The third S line was, however, opened westwards to Glostrup in 1953, and Hansen (1960) identifies a strong correlation between transport development and the growth of population and industrial jobs.

By the end of the 1950s the supply of development land from the Finger Plan was running out. In 1963 a compromise First Step Plan was adopted, based on Finger Plan principles, and extended the two southernmost fingers in steps to Køge in the south and towards Roskilde in the west. New subregional shopping centres were built at Kongens Lyngby and planned for Høje Tåstrup as services and offices followed industrial suburbanization (Diem, 1973). The 1966 Køge Bay Masterplan was for 150,000 people in 10 new suburbs from Avedøre to Jersie. Although electrification of the existing west line kept pace with the demand for urban development land, the south line needed to be constructed. Danish State Railways (DSB) chose instead to extend the north-west S line by electrifying from Holte out to Hillerød in 1968, and to develop a new S line to Farum as both routes were already populated and more profitable than the Køge line. The construction of the S line towards Køge therefore lagged several years behind housing development, reaching to Vallensbæk in 1972, Hundige in 1976, Solrød Strand in 1979 and to Jersie and Køge town in 1983, and so apartments in these suburbs were hard to let. In contrast, the government responded to the demands of car owners by 85-per-cent funding of three urban motorways through the green wedges to the north, west and south. This together with different local tax rates and housing policies in different municipalities encouraged growing social segregation, especially between the high-status northern suburbs and the lower-status Køge Bay suburbs.

A Regional Planning Council was established in 1967 and its first regional plan was adopted in 1973 to provide development land until the year 2000. Its main concept was a stronger west/east Activity Zone and a new north/south outer Activity Zone connecting together the extended fingers. Four new centres were proposed where fingers and Activity Zones intersected at Høje Tåstrup, Hammersholt, Måløv and Køge, the latter being later replaced by Greve Munde. Whereas only local plans had previously been legally enforceable, the regional plan had both the legal backing of the Urban and Rural Zones Act 1969 and the political backing of the new local-government units created in 1970 and the Metropolitan Regional Council created in 1974. This occurred, however, just as urban population growth ceased and the pressure for urban land development declined. The new Metropolitan Regional Council (HR) became a passenger transport authority on 1 April 1974, with an operating executive that enabled public-transport co-ordination and integration to occur throughout the conurbation. In October 1974, all publicly owned bus companies were merged into one owned by HR and called

Hovedstadsområdets Trafikselskab (HT). In 1975 all private bus companies became contractors for HT and zonal bus fares, and bus-rail season tickets started. In 1978 HR became financially responsible for the operation of the electrified S trains and local journeys on wider regional rail services, both still operated by DSB.

From 1979 a fully integrated zonal bus-and-train-fare system started with free transfers between all buses and trains. Co-ordination and integration resulted in 50 per cent more S-train passengers between 1977 and 1981 and 30 per cent more bus passengers by 1980. Fares covered 56 per cent of operating costs in 1980. Increased investment in railways enabled the Køge S line to be completed in 1983, electrification of the line from Ballerup to Frederikssund to form an extended S line in 1989 and main-line electrification to Helsingør in 1987 and Roskilde in 1988.

In 1982 the regional plan was downgraded as a result of population decline, but the environment was given greater emphasis. The product of over fifty years of green planning now includes the 14-km-long Vestvolden embankment footpath and cycleway of the 1960s, the West Forest, the 1980 Køge Bay Beach Park constructed on reclaimed land, the opening of reclaimed Western Amager to the public in 1984 and countless footpaths, allotments and areas of tree planting (Jensen, 1984).

In December 1989 a final and more flexible regional plan reflected the power of multinational companies to choose their own location, and also emphasized the development of many small public-transport nodes. This plan was passed days before the centre and right government abolished the Metropolitan Regional Council on 31 December but provides a framework for urban development until the mid-1990s. DSB re-acquired urban-rail financing from 1 January 1990, whilst HT bus services began to be privatized through competitive tendering to reduce soaring costs.

In the Copenhagen conurbation, integrated land use and transport planning has been based for over forty years on the principles of the 1947 Finger Plan. This has enabled a highly accessible but elongated conurbation to develop with recreation land in the form of green spaces or open country near to all residents. Delays in completing S-train lines have been overcome. Copenhagen's historic core has been preserved and traffic congestion contained. Although recent years have seen some reaction against the uniformity of housing and urban layout in some of the finger suburbs, there is little evidence (by British standards) of unlet housing or vandalism. Public services, in general, are good, and minimum living standards remain high.

4.3.2   Oslo

The Oslo/Akershus Metropolitan Region is Scandinavia's third largest urban area with a 1988 population of 847,000, an increase of 245,000 or

40.7 per cent since 1950 (Table 4.8; Figure 4.5). In 1948 the city of Oslo, Norway's capital, with a population of 275,000 in an area of only 17 km^2, had taken over the large surrounding municipality of Aker. Aker's population of nearly 140,000 was mainly suburban overspill from Oslo and had grown from only 53,000 in 1920. Its area of 436 km^2 contained many protected forests and lakes but also provided much-needed space for Oslo's growth to the east and south of the city. In the 1950s most of Oslo's population growth was in the new suburbs in Aker East and the old city's population fell sharply. By the 1960s, however, growth was larger and faster in the Near Zone and Far Zone municipalities beyond the extended city boundary. By 1970 Oslo city was losing population although the number of people living in Aker had almost doubled since 1950. Since 1970 growth has been largest in the Near Zone and fastest in the Far Zone.

Brækhus (1976) notes that Oslo Council was closely involved in controlling development in neighbouring Aker in the 1920s where Oslo's building regulations already applied. Oslo's first Master Plan of 1934 included Aker and proposed three zones of concentric urban expansion to the north and east, the north and west and the south to create a city of 700,000. For the first time the huge forest recreation area of Oslomarka was delimited to try to prevent urban encroachment (Figure 4.5). Housing

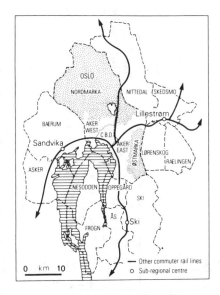
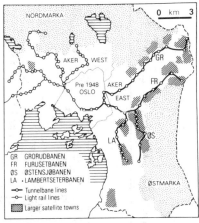

Figure 4.5   Oslo: (a) region; (b) city

Table 4.8   Oslo's population change, 1950–88 (000s)

	1950	1960	1970	1982	1988	% change 1950–70	% change 1970–88*	% change 1950–88*
1. Pre-1948 Oslo	278	221	176	146	n.a.	−36.7	−16.9	−47.4
2. Aker West	76	87	85	83	n.a.	+11.6	−2.4	+8.9
3. Aker East	75	163	204	219	n.a.	+172.3	+7.4	+192.5
4. Oslo city (1, 2 and 3)	429	471	465	448	451	+8.4	−3.0	+5.1
5. Near Zone[†]	102	145	215	249	271	+108.7	+26.0	+163.1
6. Greater Oslo (4 and 5)	531	616	680	697	722	+28.0	+6.2	+36.0
7. Far Zone[††]	71	78	97	116	125	+36.6	+29.2	+76.7
8. Oslo/Akershus Metropolitan Region (6 and 7)	602	694	777	813	847	+29.4	+9.0	+40.7
9. Rest of Norway	2,676	2,897	3,097	3,242	3,362	+15.7	+8.6	+25.6

* 1970–82 and 1950–82 for pre-1948 Oslo, Aker West and Aker East.
[†] The municipalities of Nesodden, Oppegård, Ski, Lørenskog, Rælingen, Skedsmo, Nittedal, Bærum and Asker in Akershus county.
[††] The municipalities of Frogn, Ås, Vestby, Enebakk, Aurskog-Høland, Fet, Sørum, Nes, Ullensaker, Gjerdrum and Nannestad in Akershus county and Lunner in Oppland county.
n.a. – not available.
Sources: Brækhus (1976); Rasmussen (1985); *Statistisk Årbok Norway* (1988).

development and population growth temporarily ceased during the German occupation of 1940–5.

Planning land use and transport development really began after the incorporation of Aker in 1948. In 1950 an Oslo Area Regional Planning Committee was established. The 1950 Comprehensive Plan abandoned the free-market principle of concentric urban development and inner- and core-area decline. It proposed instead a plurinuclear city with the development of subcentre satellite towns, rather than dormitory suburbs, linked to Oslo's city centre by electric railways (Rasmussen, 1965). These satellite towns were planned communities focused on a railway station with an optimal size of 14,000 people (Figure 4.5). All satellite towns contain shops and schools and many also have industrial jobs, but they are not self-sufficient in employment. Although much of the housing is in apartment blocks, fully pedestrianized neighbourhoods, internal green areas and internal green belts give each satellite town a feeling of light and space. They were developed rapidly between 1952 and 1984, mainly by the OBOS housing co-operative, and contained 200,000 people by 1990. All the satellite towns are located in the urban corridors to the east and south of Oslo except for Hovseter to the west on the Røa Light Railway. Elsewhere in the west and north, housing development has been more traditional but is mainly clustered around commercial centres and railway stations. A 1953 plan for parks, 90 km of *turveier* (green paths or hiking trails) and an Aker Valley linear park, aimed to link all parts of the urban area to Oslomarka.

A new Oslo Master Plan in 1960 was designed for a city of 600,000 people but only designated 139 km^2 for urban development, the remaining 314 km^2 forming Oslomarka, Oslo's huge recreation area of forests, lakes and streams to the north (Nordmarka) and east (Østmarka). The city's central area was to concentrate on business and commerce. Industry, previously concentrated on the harbour area and the lower Aker Valley, was decentralized so that two thirds of new industrial floorspace was in the Grorud Valley and near Østensjø. High-density inner residential areas contrasted with a variety of outer-area residential densities. A network of green paths and parks were to link the city centre and all the urban zones to the surrounding forest areas of Nordmarka and Østmarka.

The 1960 plan assumed a continued dominance of public transport but proposed the building of radial and ring roads to cater for the rapidly increasing number of private cars. It aimed to co-ordinate extensions of the T-train system with satellite-town development, which was achieved from the mid-1960s, and to connect the eastern T trains with the older, western, light-rail network by a cross city-centre tunnel, which opened in 1980.

The Building Act 1965 created a planning structure with legally binding local plans and municipal and regional plans, but they both needed special byelaws to enforce them. An Urban Renewal Act in 1967 for renovation or removal and replacement of older housing was strengthened and made effective in 1976. In 1968 a Regional Planning Board was established for Oslo and Akershus. Its 1969 Draft Regional Plan restrained further development of Oslo's three corridors of urban expansion by concentrating development in three growth centres, one in each corridor. Service-sector and industrial jobs were to be focused on Sandvika in Bærum municipality to the west, on Lillestrøm in Skedsmo municipality to the east and on Ski to the south (Figure 4.5). Journey times to Oslo were to be halved to 15 or 20 minutes by improving Norwegian State Railways' electrified commuter services (Torstenson, Metcalf and Rasmussen, 1985). A new joint Oslo and Akershus Transport Authority was established and, from 1973, the government allowed urban public-transport subsidies to be paid (Knowles, 1981). Subsidies rose to 327 million NKr by 1979. From 1980, the opening of the central Oslo tunnel allowed a through-Lillestrøm-to-Asker rapid-transit service to start. The 1969 plan extended Oslomarka beyond the city boundary to include a total area of 236,000 km^2 of forests, lakes and rivers in four counties and seventeen municipalities, providing a recreation area for one fifth of Norway's population.

From the 1970s, growing wealth enabled more people to buy cars and to live in family houses, often at great distances from Oslo in the Near or Far Zones. This choice was partly a reaction to the uniformity and overplanning of satellite towns, which were seen by many people as depersonalized and inflexible.

4.3.3   *Stockholm and other cities*

Sweden's capital, Stockholm, also saw the need for preventive rather than responsive planning. From 1904 the City Council bought up land for future development and achieved boundary extensions that enabled it to control its urban growth strongly. Stockholm sustained this control by its policy of leasing rather than selling residential land for sixty years, and industrial land for seventy five years, and its ownership of 60 per cent of the local construction industry and all trams and buses. The 1944 Masterplan established the principle of new housing areas being built by Stockholm City Council around stations on commuter rail or tram lines with major suburban centres at the end stations.

Stockholm's 1952 General Plan shows a similar relationship between planned suburban development and rapid transit development to Copenhagen's 1947 Finger Plan and Oslo's 1950 Comprehensive Plan. Stockholm's plan was more authoritarian, with a three-tier hierarchy of centres and rigidly defined pyramid density gradients declining away from each station. The 1952 plan aimed to create eighteen neighbourhoods, each with local employment, and housing a total of 250,000 people (Sidenbladh, 1965). Each neighbourhood was to be linked by radial, and mainly underground, Tunnelbana rapid transit lines to the city centre within 45 minutes. The four original Tunnelbana routes, three to the south and one to the north west, were opened between 1950 and 1960 and operating subsidies were paid from 1956. Between 1964 and 1967 two further routes opened to the south west and one to the north east with the help of 95-per-cent infrastructure grants from the government after 1964. After 1970 a second central-area tunnel route and two further Tunnelbana routes to the north west were opened. In the 1952 plan, Stockholm city centre was the A centre, whilst a B centre was built around each of eighteen Tunnelbana stations to serve a neighbourhood of about 10,000 people (Diem, 1965). C centres of three to five shops were to be located 0.5 km away from B centres to serve 3,000 to 6,000 people. D centres of one to two shops were to be located on the edge of the neighbourhood units to serve lower-density family houses. These assumed thresholds for centres were altered by the unforeseen high levels of personal wealth and private car-ownership. B centres actually required 50,000 to 100,000 people within 5 km and C centres 10,000 to 15,000 within walking distance. Regional shopping centres were built at Vällingby and Järva to the north west, Skarholmen to the south west and Högdalen and Färsta to the south. Stockholm's planned neighbourhoods failed to be self-sufficient in jobs. Vällingby, the first completed neighbourhood in 1955, had only 9,000 local jobs compared with 27,000 inhabitants by 1960 and a mere 2,000 of these jobs were taken by local people.

The 1966 Stockholm Regional Plan included an arc of land to the west for decentralized manufacturing industry. High levels of private car-ownership led to traffic congestion and a ring and radial motorway system was superimposed on the rapid-transit city. The Tunnelbana was too slow to compete in areas more than 16–21 km from the CBD. Fast, main-line commuter services provide opportunities for new neighbourhood development at greater distances to Arlanda in the north, Kungsängen in the south west and Sodertälje in the south. Greater Stockholm Passenger Transport Authority and Executive were formed in 1967 with the authority also having some land-use functions. The merger of the city and county of Stockholm also helped to integrate the planning of urban development. By 1986 Greater Stockholm was Scandinavia's second largest conurban area with a population of 1.45 million. However, since the housing shortage ended in the 1970s some of Stockholm's overplanned Tunnelbana neighbourhoods have become unpopular and vandalized, and most two-parent Swedish families with children have moved out of the apartment blocks to family houses (see section 4.2).

Greater Gothenburg is Scandinavia's fourth largest conurbation with a 1986 population of 711,000. The City Council controlled urban development in a similar way to Stockholm by purchasing land from 1878, extending the city boundaries and owning the tram and bus systems. After 1945 a light-rail system was developed by creating reserved tracks for trams, helped from 1964 by 95-per-cent government infrastructure grants. New housing estates have been developed served by extensions to the light-rail system, although only Frölunda to the south west is similar in scale to Stockholm's neighbourhood centres. All housing developments are within thirty minutes of the CBD including walking time to the light-rail stop. The creation of a Passenger Transport Authority and Executive helped to achieve co-ordination of public-transport modes and integration of land use and transport development.

All of Scandinavia's other main urban areas have grown strongly since 1950 but still have fewer than half-a-million people each. Although these urban areas all suffer from traffic congestion, the scale of the urban-development problem is much smaller so that the development of planned new suburbs is rare. Many of these towns are also underbounded and short of building land and rely on the expansion of neighbouring munici-palities to accommodate population growth. Århus is Denmark's second-largest urban area with a 1988 population of 258,000. The Århus 1966 District Plan extended existing fingers of development along radial routes from the city centre and designated two B centres at Lisbjerg and Hasselager and six C centres, one for each of the six surrounding suburban municipalities that were merged with Århus in 1970. New suburbs of high-rise apartments were built at Gjellerup to the west and Hasle to the north west. The 1975 Århus Regional Plan concentrated urban develop-ment on two rail corridors, an existing diesel commuter rail service to Malling in the south and, from 1979, a new commuter service to Hornslet, a family housing area to the north. Some bus corridors were also designated for urban development.

Greater Stavanger is now Norway's third largest urban area with a 1988 population of 197,000 – a growth of 70 per cent from its 1950 population of 115,000. It has also become more cosmopolitan as a result of oil exploitation and 7 per cent of its population are now foreigners. Stavanger city was and remains underbounded and therefore chose to develop new housing in nearly all of its existing neighbourhoods whilst space permitted (Torstenson, Metcalf and Rasmussen, 1985). Tjensvoll was, however, developed as a new satellite suburb. Stavanger acquired housing sites and developed most of them through the SBB housing co-operative, mainly at high densities. In the late 1960s an intermunicipal planning committee recommended a linear form of urban development between Stavanger and Sandnes using the Norwegian State Railway and national highway routes for commuting. The new and larger Jæren Regional Council in the late 1970s identified ten potential housing sites to the south of Stavanger.

Tromsø at 69.5°N is one of Scandinavia's many middle-sized regional towns. This size group of towns has grown fastest in the last forty years with the deconcentration and decentralization of power from national capitals and the growth of regional services, such as health and higher education. Tromsø is the regional centre for north Norway with a population over 49,000 in 1988, more than double its 1950 population of 22,500. Despite its relatively small size, Tromsø's 1976 Development Plan identifies three linear growth areas, one on Troms Island itself and others linked by bridge on Kvaløy Island and on the mainland (*ibid.*). Each linear growth area has two growth centres. Site and climatic constraints limit urban development to a maximum 50 m above sea level at this high latitude. These physical constraints encourage this linear form of discontinuous urban development.

This section has discussed the operation of land use and transport policies during a period of social harmony and rising living standards. The growth of support in Denmark and Norway for populist right-wing political parties with anti-immigration policies suggests that some of the problems of race relations in French and British cities may yet emerge in Scandinavia. The growing number of elderly people, notably in the inner cities, and the sharpened competition for funds by social welfare, health and education services may require municipal planners to make some hard choices during the 1990s.

4.4 Traffic, pedestrianization and pollution

Scandinavia's conurbations and towns all suffer from the familiar urban problems of traffic congestion, traffic accidents, airborne pollution and noise (despite the greening of urban areas) so notable, for example, in the planned development of post-war Copenhagen and Oslo. Environmental problems have increased with rapid urban-population growth but, above all, are a product of mass private car-ownership and use, industrial pollution and the switch to road freight haulage.

Widespread ownership and use of private cars has caused massive traffic congestion and has undermined post-1945 plans to rely predominantly on public transport in large urban areas. The number of private cars has risen dramatically (for example, in Oslo from 13,000 in 1948 to 179,000 in 1987 with a further 172,000 in neighbouring Akershus county). In all three countries the immediate response to urban traffic congestion in the 1950s and 1960s was to separate through traffic from local traffic by building new ring roads, bypasses and arterial roads, in some cases to motorway standard. This urban road-building programme was aided by generous government grants, 85 per cent in the case of Denmark. However, extra road capacity generated even more traffic. Other responses have been more positive. Strict control of the number, price and duration of on- and off-street car-parking places effectively regulates the number of cars using radial roads into and out of the city. In Copenhagen, the city centre is almost enclosed by the harbour and the ring of inland lakes, and access is by a limited number of roads and bridges. Strict parking controls within the city centre reduced the average daily traffic crossing the harbour from Amager Island from a 1970 peak of 150,000 down to around 130,000 in the early 1980s, and crossing the Lake Bridges from a 1967 peak of 360,000 to 190,000 in 1983.

An additional method of limiting journeys by car to the city centre is to levy an extra toll on these vehicles. Bergen introduced this additional toll in 1986, Oslo followed in 1990 and Stockholm has proposed that drivers buy a weekly public-transport ticket if they wish to use their cars in the city centre. Copenhagen's 1988 report, *Transport in the Capital*, suggested tolls for cars entering the city limits and endorsed the plan for a new S-train line under the CBD from Frederiksberg to Amager Island via Nørreport, and a new CBD station at Kongens Nytorv.

In the longer term, decentralization of employment, especially industrial employment, away from Scandinavia's city centres has reduced some of the traffic pressure. Unlike Britain and the USA, Scandinavia's strictly compatible land-use and transport zoning has enabled decentralized locations for shops, industry and offices to be easily accessible by public transport, usually rapid transit. Good examples in Greater Copenhagen are out-of-town retailing at City 1 at Lyngby and City 2 at Høje Tåstrup, industry at Glostrup and offices at Valby and Høje Tåstrup.

The separation of through vehicular traffic from local traffic enabled many Scandinavian cities and towns to remove vehicular traffic from and to pedestrianize their main shopping streets. Copenhagen was well ahead of most European cities in 1962 in removing vehicular traffic from parts of its city-centre medieval street pattern (Lemberg, 1973). Strøget, its main one-kilometre-long shopping street, was turned into a *Gå gade* or walking street. This successfully improved the shopping environment and reduced traffic accidents, air pollution and noise. Pedestrian use increased by 35 per cent to 45 per cent in five years. Only 76 per cent of Strøget's daily average 8,600 vehicles and only 38 per cent of its rush-hour vehicles reappeared in other central-area streets. The remaining trips either bypassed central Copenhagen, were diverted to public transport or were not made. Bus passengers fell by 3 per cent in the rush hour over two years but daily passengers fell by 10 per cent less than for the whole city. The same volume of goods-delivery vehicles was recorded. Noise levels on Strøget were ten to fifteen decibels below those of surrounding streets. In 1968 Fiolstræde, a secondary shopping street, was pedestrianized linking the university and cathedral area to the most heavily used S station at Nørreport. Gråbrødre Square also became a *Gå gade*. Købmagergade and three other streets were pedestrianized in 1973 to complete a network of traffic-free paved *Gå gader* across central Copenhagen.

By 1970 fourteen provincial Danish towns had pedestrian streets, most notably Ålborg, Holsterbro and Helsingør, and others followed. Many Swedish and Norwegian towns and cities also pedestrianized their main shopping streets. In other cases town centres were purpose built to separate vehicles from pedestrians, as in Stockholm's rebuilt city centre and its new Tunnelbana regional and neighbourhood centres, Oslo's satellite towns and Copenhagen's finger towns.

Because of Oslo's fjordhead location, several national highways cannot avoid its inner-city area. In 1973 Oslo's Gatebruksplan (street-use plan) restricted car use especially in the rush hour, reduced parking, improved walking and cycling facilities and gave public transport priority over cars. By 1979 most of Karl Johansgate, Oslo's main street, and a network of side streets were pedestrianized with an underground T-train station in the heart of the CBD from 1980. The modal split for the 200,000 daily journeys to Oslo city centre in 1979 was 54 per cent by public transport, 31 per cent by car and 15 per cent by bicycle, which shows a sharp fall in car use since 1969.

Growing public concern for the local environment has led to tighter controls on waste disposal, on noise and on pollution from industry, transport, power stations and central-heating boilers (see Chapter 2, section 2.4). Catalytic convertors are compulsory on all new cars and lead-free petrol is widely used, but cars are still a major source of pollution. Cars are heavily taxed in Scandinavia to reduce demand. For example, the 200-per-cent tax on all new cars in Denmark triples their purchase price. Between February 1980 and February 1988, sulphur-dioxide emissions were substantially reduced in Scandinavia's urban areas. Levels fell, for example, from 113 to 27 microgrammes per m^3 in Stockholm, 82 to 28 in Oslo, 55 to 25 in Copenhagen, 60 to 32 in Gothenburg, 73 to 15 in Malmö, 39 to 8 in Bergen, 36 to 7 in Trondheim and 78 to 2 in Umeå. Swedish statistics show that virtually all of this reduction was a result of better controls on industry and power stations. Urban dust and lead levels have also fallen in recent years.

FIVE

Social Democracy and the Welfare State

The four cornerstones of Scandinavian social democracy are full employment, a comprehensive Welfare State, redistribution of income through a progressive taxation system and a regional development policy to reduce spatial inequality. The Welfare State provides a universal, free, State-education system, a national health service, social services and a safety net against poverty. Neither capitalist nor State socialist, Scandinavian social democracy has been proclaimed as the third way to develop advanced societies and economies. In contrast to Britain, social democracy in Scandinavia preferred regulation of privately owned industry to widespread State ownership.

5.1 Full employment

A social-democratic consensus emerged in each country in 1945 after the traumas of world war, of German occupation of Denmark and Norway and of mass unemployment in the 1920s and 1930s. In Norway, for example, the all-party Joint Programme for Reconstruction in 1945 'became the cornerstone of Norway's emerging welfare state structure' (Rasmussen, 1985, p. 260). The joint programme stated (*ibid.* pp. 262–3) that

> All who are able to work shall have the right and obligation to employment. ... No unemployment must be tolerated. ... The essential tasks for our economy and all economic activities in the country are to provide jobs for everyone ... to create a just and fair distribution of the results and provide good living conditions for everyone.

Full employment was later incorporated as a new paragraph into Norway's constitution in 1954. Despite the election of non-socialist centre and right governments in Norway in 1965, Denmark in 1968 and Sweden in 1976, the social-democratic, Keynesian consensus was maintained for State action to sustain full employment (Figure 5.1). Only in the 1980s, and especially since the formation of more right-wing governments in Denmark in 1988 and in Norway from 1989–90, has this consensus been challenged but not yet broken.

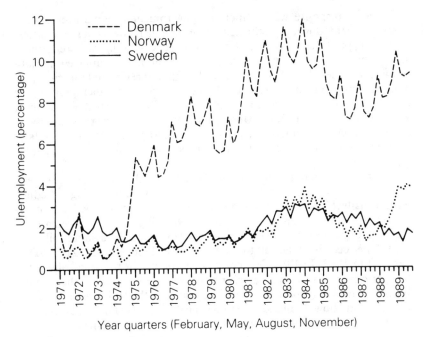

Year quarters (February, May, August, November)

Figure 5.1 Unemployment, 1971–89

During the relatively rapid economic growth up to 1973, the development of industrial economies with full employment was achieved without much difficulty. Commercialization of agriculture, forestry and fishing led to widespread labour shedding in rural areas and rural-to-urban migration to find work in the expanding manufacturing industries and service sector. A growing labour shortage from the mid-1960s resulted in a peak of 300,000 Finns working temporarily in Sweden in 1970 under the five-nation Nordic Common Labour Policy. Sweden, Denmark and Norway also experienced a less substantial immigration of south European and Asian labour, largely employed in lower-paid unskilled and semi-skilled jobs. Full employment, defined as less than 2-per-cent unemployment, was threatened by the Organization of Petroleum Exporting Countries (OPEC) oil price rises of 1973–4 and 1979, which brought high inflation, lower economic growth and, in the latter case, international recession. This period coincided with the much larger post-war cohorts reaching adult age and a much greater proportion of women seeking work.

Sweden's response was to increase government expenditure to keep unemployment down by subsidizing or nationalizing ailing industries, expanding public services and public works, encouraging early retirement and setting up job-training schemes. The number employed in job-training schemes alone soon exceeded the number registered unemployed. The full employment threshold of under 2 per cent unemployed was breached continuously from late 1981 until 1987 as government support was reduced (Figure 5.1). Unemployment in Sweden remains above average among the under-25s, women, non-Europeans and inhabitants of the seven northern forest counties, and shows a seasonal high in mid-winter.

Denmark's economy was facing the additional rigours of European Community (EC) membership from 1973, and was also trying to reduce its unusually high dependence on imported fuel. Denmark has not achieved full employment since summer 1974 (Figure 5.1). Average unemployment climbed to 7.3 per cent in 1978 and, after a slight fall, rose to 10.5 per cent in 1983, fell to 7.8 per cent in 1986 and rose again to 9.5 per cent in 1989. In 1988 Denmark's unemployment remained above the 8.7-per-cent national average among the under-35s, women, the foreign-born population (especially non-Europeans, with 31.4 per cent unemployed) and shows a marked seasonal peak in mid-winter. The regional variation was between 11.3 per cent unemployed in Nordjyllands county and Copenhagen city and 5.6 per cent in Frederiksborg and Copenhagen counties. Since the mid-1970s, regional unemployment has been above average in Nordjyllands, Århus, Fyns, Bornholms, Vestsjællands and Storstrøms counties and Copenhagen city. After the mid-1970s the previous unemployment blackspots of west and south Jutland benefited from their close proximity to the rest of the EC, with average or below-average unemployment.

Norway's economy in the 1970s was unique as its enormous oil and gas revenues enabled the rapid expansion of the 1950s and 1960s to continue with full employment. However, a large share of government revenue was spent maintaining employment in uncompetitive manufacturing, agricultural and fisheries jobs and also in the marginal regions, particularly north Norway. In the early 1980s the new centre and right government reduced its spending and 2 per cent unemployment was exceeded between summer 1982 and spring 1986. The oil-price crash in 1986 from $30 to $11 a barrel reduced government revenues and lowered the value of Norway's currency, which helped international competitiveness. The 1986 Social Democratic minority government was eventually forced to cut back its employment subsidies and unemployment rose sharply to 2.3 per cent in 1988 and 3.8 per cent in 1989. The new centre and right government, elected in September 1989, inherited a worsening situation, with unemployment reaching a record 4.9 per cent in January and July 1990 — with a further 2.8 per cent and 1.3 per cent respectively engaged on unemployment relief schemes. Norway's unemployment remains above average for the under-25s, for women and in the marginal regions of north Norway and the west coast north of Bergen. Finnmark county, with the collapse of cod fishing, and Hordaland county, are the unemployment blackspots. In January 1991 unemployment reached a new record of 5.2 per cent with a further 2.1 per cent on government employment schemes.

Problems with unemployment in the last twenty years should not obscure the fact that between 1972 and 1988 the total number of persons in employment increased by 28 per cent in Norway, 14 per cent in Sweden and 12 per cent in Denmark (Table 5.1). Women account for almost all of this increase in employment in Denmark and Sweden, and three quarters of it in Norway. Most of these new jobs are in the service sector, many of them part time in health and social services. They reflect a remarkably rapid rise in the proportion of women aged between 15 and 74 who are in work. From 1972 to 1988 this female activity rate rose from 53.5 per cent to 68.5 per cent in Denmark, 44.8 per cent to 63.7 per cent in Norway and 54.7 per cent to over 70 per cent in Sweden, which is the highest in the Western world. Male activity rates in comparison have been fairly steady at around or just below 80 per cent. In the 15–25 age-group the difference between male and female activity rates is even less and is almost equal in Sweden.

5.2 The changing role of women

The transformation of the role of women in Scandinavian society extends from political life to public child care, employment, separate taxation and parental leave, and is well ahead of other Western countries. All five Nordic countries have been more committed to equality and solidarity, reflected in advanced social policies and a greater degree of equality with men in income and education. The gender differences remain widest in Norway (Haavio-Mannila *et al.*, 1985). The ability of women to choose a different role has been enhanced by sex education and effective contraception, and by the availability of legal free abortion in Denmark since 1970, in Sweden since 1975 and in Norway since 1978.

Women MPs account for 131 out of 349 (37.5 per cent) in the Swedish Riksdag elected in 1988, 59 out of 165 (35.8 per cent) in the Norwegian Storting elected in 1989 and 55 out of 175 (31.4 per cent) in the Danish Folketing elected in 1988. Women membership of county and municipal councils is often higher, especially in metropolitan areas, with a majority first achieved in Norway in 1971 in the 'Women's Coup' on Oslo,

Table 5.1 Employment and activity rates, 1972–88

	1972			1979			1983			1988		
	Male	Female	Total	Male	Female	Total	Male	Female	Total	Male	Female	Total
Denmark												
Employment (000s)	1,436	965	2,401	1,439	1,090	2,529	1,322	1,088	2,410	1,465	1,221	2,686
Activity rate (%)	80.8	53.5	67.1	79.3	60.9	70.1	78.4	64.7	71.5	81.0	68.5	74.8
Norway												
Employment (000s)	1,048	601	1,649	1,110	762	1,872	1,127	818	1,945	1,173	941	2,114
Activity rate (%)	78.2	44.8	61.4	78.2	54.2	66.2	78.5	57.6	68.1	78.3	63.7	71.1
Sweden												
Employment (000s)	2,295	1,567	3,862	2,315	1,865	4,180	2,258	1,966	4,224	2,287	2,112	4,399
Activity rate (%)	79.7	54.7	67.2	78.5	63.5	71.0	76.7	66.9	71.8	86.2*	81.8*	84.0*

* As a %, 16–64. Elsewhere 15–74, Denmark; 16–74, Norway and Sweden.
Source: *Yearbook of Nordic Statistics* (1981 and 1989–90)

Trondheim and Asker's municipal councils (Sinkkonen, 1985). However, women often still have less power and influence than representation, although since 1976, 25–30 per cent of all Swedish cabinet posts have been held by women and ten Scandinavian political parties have minimum quotas for women in party office, usually 40 per cent. Gro Harlem Brundtland became Norway's, and Scandinavia's, first woman Prime Minister in 1981, from 1986 to 1989 and again from November 1990, choosing cabinets in 1986 and 1990 with half women and half men. There is an increasing gender gap in political allegiance with gender taking precedence over traditional left and right family allegiances. A majority of women vote Social Democrat or for other left parties, rising to 64 per cent of women under 30 in Denmark's 1984 Folketing election. In single-issue politics, such as the question of Swedish nuclear power, women and men are equally involved. The 1987 Swedish Commission on Women's Representation recommended a 30-per-cent female representation on national directorates, official commissions, committees and boards by 1992, and 50-per-cent representation by 1998. Since 1988, Norway's Equal Status Act requires all committees, boards and councils appointed or elected by public agencies or institutions to have at least 40-per-cent representation of both sexes if they have four or more members, with both sexes represented on committees with two or three members.

Women still, however, have little control in the labour market. Managers and leaders of trade unions and employers organizations are nearly all men. In Landorganisationen i Danmark (LO – the Federation of Danish Trade Unions), for example, women form half the membership but only 20 per cent of the leadership (Hansen, Ryding and Borre, 1985). A notable exception is the Danish all-female Kvindeligt Arbejder Forbund (Union of Women Workers), which is unique in Scandinavia. This general under-representation of women in positions of power and control is partly attributed to the constraints and costs of child-care provision, part-time employment in a mainly gender-segregated labour market and caring for sick children, children on school holidays and elderly relatives (Hernes and Hänninen-Salmelin, 1985; Showstack-Sassoon, 1987).

The question of justice and equality between women and men has become part of the Scandinavian political agenda. The concept of an equal-opportunities policy is accepted across the political spectrum in Scandinavia with Equal Status Councils established in Norway and Sweden in 1972 and Denmark in 1975. Acts of Parliament were passed in Denmark on equal pay and equal treatment in 1976, and in Norway on equal status in employment, pay and education in 1978. However, the implementation of equal opportunities is furthest advanced in Sweden. Sweden's Equal Opportunities Act 1980 promotes equal rights for women and men in employment, working conditions and opportunities for development at work. The Act also bans gender discrimination and empowers the Equal Opportunities Ombudsman and the Equal Opportunities Commission (Eduards, 1989). In the 1960s, joint taxation of married women penalized working wives. Separate taxation from 1971 equalized the tax rates for married and unmarried people except for a small 1,800 SKr tax deduction for a stay-at-home wife or husband.

Public child care helps both parents to work and, in the early 1970s, there was a large expansion of Swedish municipal day-care centres for pre-school children to enable 'employment for all' to be a realistic opportunity. Day-care centres are open from 7 a.m. to 6 p.m. but are used mainly on a part-time basis. By 1988, 85 per cent of Swedish mothers with pre-school children and 92 per cent with children aged 7–16 worked, half of them part time. In 1986 the full-time costs of a public day-centre place were shared 53 per cent by the municipality, 32 per cent by central government and 15 per cent by parents. No public financial support is given to private day-care centres, which is the alternative policy favoured by the centre and right parties.

Since 1974 the Swedish parental insurance system has helped either parent to stay at home by currently providing twelve months loss-of-earnings compensation, to be extended gradually in future to eighteen months. Nine months compensation is at 90 per cent of previous earned income and the scheme can be taken up at any time up to the child's fourth birthday. Parents of infant children have also been entitled, since 1979, to a six-hour working day. Additional pension points have been given since 1982 for looking after children in the home.

The outcome of Sweden's generous child support is not gender neutral, however, as only 6 per cent of parental insurance benefits are claimed by men. Therefore, there is still a substantial gap between men and women's earnings and socioeconomic conditions, although women's aspirations to have children and the opportunity to work have been fulfilled to a greater extent than in any other democracy.

Throughout Scandinavia the changing aspirations and role of women have resulted in dramatic changes in family life. More people live alone, especially in Denmark and Sweden, as a result of a sharp fall in marriages and an even sharper rise in divorces. In 1983 there were as many single as married adults in Denmark. The birth rate has fallen and, throughout Scandinavia, has stabilized below replacement level, as women have chosen education, work, greater personal freedom and sometimes a higher standard of living instead of more children (Hansen, Rying and Borre, 1985). By 1983, one fifth of Danish families with children formed single-parent households, with many on low incomes or welfare support.

5.3 Education

Education is given very high priority in Scandinavia and forms the largest single area of government expenditure. In Norway, for example, its education expenditure of 40 billion NKr in 1987 represented 7.8 per cent of gross national product (GNP) (Ministry of Church and Education, 1989). In all three countries there are nine years of compulsory 'basic' education from the ages of 7 to 16, with two semesters each year. This basic State education is free to the user and includes free school meals and free transport beyond a certain distance, which is 4 km in Norway. For pupils from remote rural areas, residential facilities are provided free for weekly or termly boarding. Basic education is comprehensive and mixed ability to ensure that all children receive the same general education. Equal-opportunity policies positively attempt to break down male and female stereotypes.

Linguistic minorities are treated generously. In Sweden, for example, all pupils from non-Swedish speaking households are entitled both to learn Swedish, initially as a foreign language, and to mother-tongue teaching at public expense (Swedish Institute, 1987). There are two Norwegian languages, Bokmål, derived from Danish, which is the principal language of the larger towns and of south-east and north Norway, and Nynorsk, derived from country dialects, which is the main language of south and west Norway. Basic school-children learn to read both languages and each municipality decides which language is to be used for written instruction. All books are produced at equal price in both languages to protect Nynorsk. In north and central Norway the Sami minority have been entitled, since 1985, to receive all basic education in Sami, which is a Finno-Ugrian language unrelated to Norwegian (Stange, 1990).

Since the 1970s handicapped children have been integrated, where possible, into ordinary schools, although some State- or county-run special schools remain. Only a tiny proportion of pupils attend private schools in Norway and Sweden, although in Norway private schools with special education philosophies, such as Steiner schools, are State supported. However, in Denmark, where the State pays 85 per cent of private school's running costs, 10 per cent of pupils attend private basic schools.

Facilities for under-7s vary considerably within Scandinavia, but are not considered to be part of the education system. In Denmark, 44 per cent of children from birth to 2 years are in nurseries and full-time centres, and 87 per cent of 3–6-year-olds are in kindergartens or pre-school centres. Pre-school facilities are even better in Sweden, with all children entitled to at least one year as part of public child care. In

Norway, however, only 30 per cent of pre-school children are in kinder-gartens although Norway is likely to lower the school starting age to 6 during the 1990s.

The organization of State education is similar in each country. Basic education is run by the municipalities and, in Norway and Sweden, consists of six years of primary education from the ages of 7 to 13 and three years of lower secondary education from the ages of 13 to 16. In Denmark, basic school runs straight through from ages 7 to 16 (Ministry of Education, 1990). Municipalities are divided into school districts with one primary or basic school per district, and about 18 pupils per class. In sparsely populated rural areas schools are very small. Norway has 1,000 primary schools that are too small for one class per year and a further 270 schools with only one class overall. The minimum school size of six pupils is not always enforced for political reasons, and in 1988–9 there were 52 primary schools in Norway with fewer than six pupils (Stange, 1990). Lower secondary schools are usually larger, normally with two or three parallel classes of about 23 pupils each but, in some rural areas, long distances necessitate primary schools retaining these age-groups.

Each country has a national curriculum for basic education with English compulsory from year 3 or 4, although in Denmark and Norway the national curriculum forms more of an outline with the detail delegated to schools. In order to deliver the same level of education in all areas of Scandinavia, governments have had to offer financial inducements to attract teachers to remoter areas and small islands. In 1987 Norway enhanced these incentives for its northernmost county, Finnmark.

The last thirty years have witnessed a huge expansion in post-compulsory education in Scandinavia, especially among females. Over 90 per cent of 16-year-old children choose to continue with upper secondary schooling for between one and four years but normally for three years. These vocational and academic schools offer a wide variety of courses and are usually located in towns and cities. Academic upper secondary schools, called *Gymnasia*, are run by the municipalities in Sweden and by the counties in Denmark and Norway, although in Sweden State-funded county education committees provide advisory services, in-service training and supervision. In Denmark commercial and technical schools are private foundations with courses funded by the government.

Folk High Schools are a distinctive alternative form of residential education in Scandinavia. First established in Denmark in 1844 by N.F.S. Grundtvig, the Danish theologian, poet and historian to educate farming families, they soon spread throughout Scandinavia. Folk High Schools concentrate on personal development with immersion in literature, history and a wide range of other subjects. These schools have no entrance qualification or leaving examinations or qualifications for their mixture of full-year and short courses. There are currently over 100 Folk High Schools in Denmark, 80 in Norway and 125 in Sweden.

From the age of 19 a large proportion of Scandinavians, 35 per cent in the case of Sweden, enrol in State-funded further and higher education with an equal proportion of males and females. Most enter one of a variety of colleges to obtain vocational qualifications, with the rest taking university degrees in a greatly expanded higher-education system. Bachelors degrees take from 3.5 to 4 years of study and master degrees from 5 to 7 years, often spread out over a longer period. Students live off a combination of grants and interest-bearing loans, whose repayment burdens them for much of adult life. Most higher education is provided in larger towns and cities, which have grown accordingly. This also results in a brain-drain from rural areas as highly skilled professional or technical jobs are seldom found outside urban areas. Indeed, it has been government policy to decentralize higher education from the metropolitan areas by expanding or creating such facilities in regional centres in order to strengthen them. Norway upgraded Trondheim's higher-education facilities to university status in 1969 and opened Tromsø University in Arctic Norway in 1972 to add to the established universities in Oslo and Bergen. Since 1969, fourteen new State-funded regional colleges have opened throughout Norway, each with different specialisms, and regional college boards have been established in all eighteen counties. These are additional to previously established vocational and teacher-training colleges. Denmark has also opened many colleges, a technical university at Lyngby, and two new universities in Odense in 1966 and Roskilde in 1970 to complement the long-established universities in Copenhagen and Århus. Sweden, with universities already in Uppsala, Lund, Gothenburg and Stockholm, has added new universities at Umeå in north Sweden in 1963 and at Linköping in 1970, as well as seventeen university colleges in twenty towns to cover all of Sweden's 24 counties. Sweden also has a wide variety of vocational colleges (Swedish Institute, 1989a). Distance learning is also an important new facility for many rural dwellers in Norway, whilst adult education is both widespread and popular throughout Scandinavia.

5.4 Health and social services

The Scandinavian social-democratic Welfare State has placed great emphasis on guaranteeing all citizens good standards of physical and material well-being and social and economic equality (Hernes, 1988). Each Scandinavian country has a National Health Service, which gives free access to general medical practitioners and hospitals. Medicines and dental treatment are free to children and subsidized for adults (Royal

Danish Ministry of Health, 1987). The health service is mainly financed by local government through local income tax. General hospitals are run on a county level in Scandinavia, although specialist hospitals are located regionally or nationally. In Sweden, six health regions, each with over 1 million people, are based on the medical schools and the research, teaching and specialist hospitals based at Stockholm, Gothenburg, Uppsala, Lund, Linköping and Umeå (Swedish Institute, 1989b). Primary health-care services are run at municipality level in Sweden and Norway and at county level in Denmark, although Danish municipalities run some local health services, such as home nurses, infant health visitors and school health and dental services. Since 1957, all Nordic countries have granted reciprocal rights to other Nordic citizens resident in their country for all social-welfare and public-health services.

Scandinavia's health services provide high-quality health care to all, regardless of income. They have, together with better nutrition and housing, helped to raise average life expectancy by eliminating the great epidemic diseases, such as smallpox, by curing or preventing serious illnesses (such as tuberculosis and pneumonia) and by reducing infant mortality to well under 1 per cent. Scandinavian women born in the late 1980s can expect to live, on average, to 80 years of age in Sweden and Norway, and 78 in Denmark, whilst men can expect to live, on average, to 74, 73 and 72 respectively. This represents an average increase in lifespan of nine years for women and five years for men compared to Scandinavians born in the 1940s.

The number of pensioners, aged 67 or above, has risen sharply, more than doubling, for example, in Norway from 1950 to 1980. This has placed additional pressure on health services, national pension schemes and social services. Scandinavia's social services are provided by the local municipalities. Apart from ensuring financial, social, physical and mental security, social services aim to promote activity and participation by assisting people to remain in the community rather than in institutions. Housing grants or cheap improvement loans help the elderly, handicapped and poor to improve their homes. Home helps, home nursing, social-service centres and day centres for the elderly help the old and infirm to retain their independence. Sheltered housing provides more supervision without the cost, and the institutionalization of residential and nursing homes remains necessary for the minority of people unable to look after themselves.

Now, after half a century's growth, this 'cradle to the grave' Welfare State is in crisis throughout Scandinavia. The secure *Folkhem* (people's home) created by the Social Democrats and developed through a long period of social-democratic consensus, has become too expensive even for the community-minded and conformist Swedes.

The increased real cost and take-up of modern health and medical care and social services, together with generous child-care facilities, maternity, paternity, sickness and unemployment benefits and an ageing population, have all contributed to the massive personal tax burden. Per-capita public-health and social-welfare expenditure, for example, rose in real terms between 1978 and 1987 by 14.3 per cent in Denmark to DKr 55,931, by 40.2 per cent in Norway to NKr 55,651 and by 29.8 per cent in Sweden to SKr 65,285 (*Yearbook of Nordic Statistics,* 1989–90). In Sweden alone, the number of health-care employees has risen from 115,000 in 1960 (representing 3 per cent of the total workforce) to 450,000 by 1987, or 10 per cent of the total workforce (Swedish Institute, 1989b). Many of these new jobs are part time and occupied by women whose employment life-cycle is often discontinuous because of the constraints of child rearing and other unpaid service work. The Swedish National Health Service is Europe's most expensive, absorbing 10 per cent of gross domestic product (GDP), whilst failing to eliminate waiting lists for certain operations. Schierbeck (1990) observes that Swedish employees now report themselves sick three times more often than in 1969, with a current annual average of 29.8 sick days for women and 22.5 for men. In 1989 Sweden's tax burden was equal to 57 per cent of GDP – an increase of 20 per cent in twenty years and easily the highest figure for any advanced economy.

Scandinavian reactions to this tax burden include tax avoidance and the growth of far-right political parties in Denmark and Norway advocating low taxes and public expenditure cuts. The 'black' economy is growing in Scandinavia, particularly among the young, with people paying cash for services and not declaring cash income for tax purposes. New far-right Progress Parties have exploited the welfare consensus of the old established social democratic, centre and right political parties, and have gained support so that they currently form Norway's third largest, and Denmark's fifth largest, parliamentary groups. The Progress Parties campaign to slash public expenditure (in Norway's case from 50 per cent to 30 per cent), they exploit abuses and shortcomings of the social-welfare system and advocate more restrictive immigration policies. Even Norway's small Christian Democratic Party, which draws support from strict rural Lutheran areas, has condemned as heartless the Progress Party's demand for tougher controls on social-security payments to single mothers. Neither the Danish nor the Norwegian Progress Party has been allowed into government, even though they have often held a numerical balance of power in parliament between the social-democratic and traditional centre and right groups. In both 1986 and 1990 Norway's centre and right minority governments have preferred to hand over power to minority social-democratic governments rather than include the far right.

However, policy changes have occurred. A freeze on further expansion of Denmark's Welfare State resulted in a budget surplus in 1986. The emphasis has shifted in Denmark away from the concept of the social welfare system towards the needs of the individual person. In Sweden, the 1990 alliance between the opposition Conservative and Liberal Parties, with policies to reduce public expenditure, threatens to end the Social Democrats' long rule since 1932 with only one six-year gap. The government responded with 5 billion SKr cuts in public expenditure. The earlier Conservative, Liberal and Centre Party 1987 agreement on private child-care allowances, as an alternative to the Social Democrats' expensive State child-care provision, showed that distinctive and lower-cost welfare policies were possible.

5.5   Regional development problems and policies

5.5.1   Scandinavia

After a long period of rationalization and commercialization of agriculture, fisheries and forestry, the primary sector is no longer the major reason for regional inequalities in Denmark, Norway and Sweden. Scandinavia's regional development problems in the 1990s relate mainly to crises in locally dominant or large industries that operate in small and often isolated labour markets.

The emphasis for the 1990s is on counties developing competitive self-reliance, which fits in with the national philosophies of intense specialization and free trade and the decentralization of more power to county level. The health and stability of the national economy is, however, paramount, and is recognized as a prerequisite for any regional policy. More support is therefore now given to research and development, especially in Sweden, and to education and training to create productive opportunities and a skilled labour force for the future.

The basic economic, rather than social and cultural, argument to support a regional policy is that it can create the conditions for a more viable and efficient industrial system to develop. There are also important strategic reasons for maintaining population and economic activity in northern Norway and Sweden and on Danish islands such as Bornholm. However, regional policy in the 1990s continues to reflect the needs of the 1960s as it is still mainly directed to the restructuring of primary activities where labour shedding is now almost complete, and to a much reduced regional divide − north−south in Norway and Sweden, and west−east in Denmark. Each country has experienced a diminishing gap in per-capita incomes between counties because of a decline in the number of lower-paid primary-sector jobs, and national wage policies that favour low-income groups. All three countries apply progressive income tax so that after-tax differences are even less. The relationship between income and actual standard of living is also weakened by a strong informal economy in non-metropolitan areas, involving unpaid exchange of services and growing food, hunting and fishing for own consumption, as well as the higher cost of housing and transport in metropolitan areas.

Regional development and economic restructuring was achieved relatively easily from the 1950s to the OPEC oil-price rise in 1973, as Scandinavia experienced high employment and fast economic growth, and international trade grew strongly with lower tariff barriers and increased demand resulting from EFTA and General Agreement on Tariffs and Trade (GATT) membership. Regional policy included upgrading the infrastructure to the standard of the core area, inducing industry to relocate or expand in development areas and subsidizing or restructuring existing industry that was at risk. As manufacturing became more footloose, much of the regional development aid was directed to new firms that were not resource based. Northern Norway and Sweden nevertheless remained highly dependent on resource-based industries. Since the mid-1960s employment in manufacturing industry has declined overall and deconcentrated, even at a county level. The metropolitan areas have experienced the strongest employment decline in manufacturing and a boom in production related and other services, as part of a rapid transition to a post-industrial economy in which the service sector dominates.

Since 1973, developments in international trade, especially competition from south-east Asia, have made Scandinavia's regional problems worse. Slower economic growth has also limited the ability of government to respond. A particular Scandinavian problem is that industrial specialization as a result of the availability of local raw materials or cheap hydropower can lead to the overdependence of an area on a single industry. When the dominant firm faces closure in a one-industry town, the government is placed under enormous political pressure to provide subsidies to prevent high, local unemployment. Shipbuilding has posed problems for all three countries, northern iron-ore mining, steel and textiles for Norway and Sweden, some fish processing for Norway and some pulp and paper processing for Sweden. Although northern Norway and northern Sweden have the largest development problems in Scandinavia and the bulk of specific regional aid, subsidies to agriculture, fisheries and ailing industries are much greater and are concentrated elsewhere.

In addition to regional policy on a national scale, the Nordic Council organizes regional policy co-operation among all five Nordic countries through the Nordic Committee on Regional Policy (NARP). Particular emphasis has been placed on co-operation in Nordkalotten, the northern areas of Norway, Sweden and Finland, in Øresund between the Greater Copenhagen and Greater Malmö areas of Denmark and Sweden, and in the Mid-Nordic area of Norway, Sweden and Finland between 62° N and 64° N. Research into regional policy is co-ordinated by the NordREFO Institute.

5.5.2   Denmark

A marked change occurred in the early 1970s in Denmark's regional population development. For many decades, Copenhagen and the urban areas of east Jutland had attracted heavy net inmigration from rural Denmark, most notably from west Jutland. This reflected the surplus of rural births, the decline in demand for rural labour with the mechanization of farming and the availability of urban job opportunities, especially in manufacturing in Copenhagen.

In the 1970s, Denmark's birth rate fell sharply and rural labour-shedding virtually ceased. At the same time, urban-based manufacturing began to shed labour quickly, whilst the service sector and unemployment increased. As a result, net migration patterns reversed, albeit at a lower level, with net gains in peripheral counties, large net losses from Metropolitan Copenhagen and smaller losses from the urban areas of east Jutland. Counterurbanization was occurring in Denmark (Court, 1987).

Population stability became the norm in the 1980s as peripheral regions ceased growing and the main urban areas halted their migration losses. The westward shift in employment since 1970 can be explained by thriving agricultural exports to the EC and more modern industries in Jutland, and more decentralized local services, as well as by declining old industries and a cut-back in higher-order public services, especially in Copenhagen.

The regional-planning response has changed from a capital city to a national perspective. The 1947 Finger Plan channelled Copenhagen's urban growth into five transport corridors or fingers radiating from the urban core. The 1963 First Step Plan extended the south-west finger to Køge and the west finger towards Roskilde. The 1962 Zone Plan for Denmark led to the Urban and Rural Zones Act 1969, which extended land-use planning to the whole of Denmark (Toft-Jensen, 1982). County reform in 1965 had reduced the number of counties from 25 to 14, while municipal reform in 1970 reduced the number of municipalities from 1,388 to 277. This created counties and municipalities of sufficient size to receive decentralized powers and provide local services. The National and Regional Planning Act 1973 provided a statutory framework for the promotion of economic and social development throughout Denmark to provide reasonable access to education, employment and services. This required the provision of services and stimulation of employment in smaller settlements. Decentralization was aided by the new counties and Greater Copenhagen becoming responsible for regional planning. The 1972 Greater Copenhagen Strategic Structure Plan and a series of Regional Plans from 1973 onwards restricted urban development to the western and southern sections of the Metropolitan Region.

In Denmark, the relatively small differences in regional unemployment and wealth had delayed the introduction of government regional development policy until 1958. Financial incentives were then used to stimulate the creation of manufacturing jobs in peripheral areas with little industry. Since the early 1970s, more emphasis has been placed on the service-sector and small-growth centres. Direct government investment has been limited to a few schemes, such as the creation of Hanstholm new town in north-west Jutland in 1968, new universities at Odense and Ålborg and inter-regional bridge, tunnel and road links. In addition, the Greenland Trading Company was moved from Copenhagen to Ålborg. The particular problem of rapid population decline on many of the one-hundred inhabited islands was addressed by government ferry subsidies from 1975 on routes where bridges were not technically or economically feasible, and by government support for island business and social projects from 1983.

During the 1970s Danish unemployment grew sharply, especially with deindustrialization in Copenhagen. In contrast, some traditional unemployment blackspots in south and west Jutland prospered, with unemployment falling below the national average. As the economic pre-eminence of Copenhagen has declined, the need for far-reaching regional development and planning policies has receded. In the late 1980s the more free-market philosophy of the centre and right government led to the abolition of the 16-year-old Greater Copenhagen Council at the end of 1989. However, it left as a legacy its latest Regional Plan 1989–2001, which retained the principles of the original 1947 Finger Plan.

Since 1988, government regional development areas have been reduced from 24.1 per cent to 19.9 per cent of the national population, including priority areas down from 15.7 per cent to 11.1 per cent (Bachtler and Bienkowski, 1988). Regional development areas are designated on the basis of eligible municipalities, which creates a patchwork of development status (Figure 5.2). Priority regions, with maximum investment grants of 35 per cent, are geographically peripheral, confined to parts of Nordjyllands county, part of the German borderland, the whole of the remote Baltic island county of Bornholm, most of the islands in the Kattegat and south of Fyn, and the western part of Lolland. Ordinary regions, with maximum investment grants of 25 per cent, include the rest of Nordjyllands county, the north-west and south-west coasts of Jutland, the Jutland coast north of Århus, most of Lolland and newly designated areas in western Fyn.

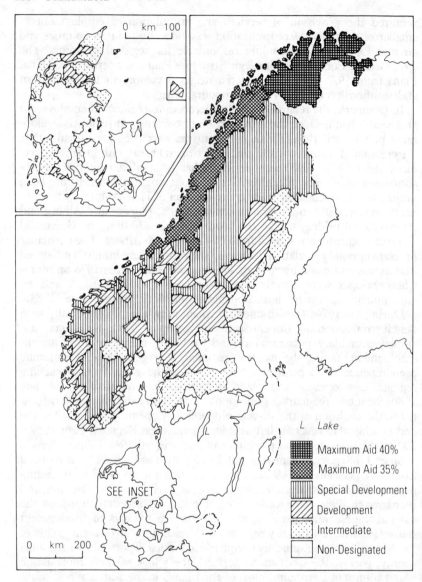

Figure 5.2 Regional development areas, 1990

Other policy changes in 1988 included targeting regional-development investment grants and loans on new productive activity, clawback of grants from commercially successful projects, support for technological development and export promotion, technical centres and consultancy work, as well as the creation of support centres for small and medium-sized firms. In contrast to Britain's regional policy, Danish regional aid is additional to European aid. The more discretionary emphasis in Danish regional development policy is linked to government financial cutbacks and the value-for-money requirement to prove the need for assistance and the fundamental impact on the local or regional economy.

5.5.3 *Norway*

Norway has experienced marked disparities in regional development as a result of a limited and scattered resource base. Industrialization was delayed by the lack of indigenous coal supplies. Although hydro-electricity provided a later source of energy for industry, it could not at first be commercially transmitted over long distances so that decentralized urbanization occurred and many one-industry towns were created at remote waterfall locations, such as Rjukan and Årdal. Rapid rationalization of primary employment in agriculture, fisheries and forestry from a largely subsistence to a largely commercial base caused regional problems in the peripheral areas of coastal and inland Norway in the 1950s and 1960s, as primary employment fell from over 30 per cent to under 10 per cent. This in turn led to a heavy outmigration of surplus rural labour from all regions of Norway to the most heavily urbanized counties bordering the Oslofjord in the south east around the capital, Oslo.

Norway's regional development-planning response began in 1949 with the creation of county planning offices in Nordland, Troms and Finnmark, the three counties of north Norway. North Norway had the weakest resource base, the greatest dependence on primary employment, the lowest income levels, the highest unemployment and the greatest distances to foreign and Norwegian markets. It also suffered most war damage as the town of Bodø had been bombed in 1940 and all buildings in Finnmark and east Troms had been razed to the ground by the retreating German army in 1945. The settlement pattern was recreated *in situ*, foregoing the opportunity to regroup settlement in line with the needs of a modern economy. By 1959 all counties in Norway had established economic planning offices.

Norway's regional development programme began in 1952 in north Norway and was extended in 1958 to the coastal districts of Trøndelag and north Møre. These programmes concentrated on improving the transport infrastructure by building new roads, bridges, vehicle ferry links and airports, as well as developing manufacturing industry and hydro-electric power. Outmigration increased from peripheral counties but population continued to grow because of high birth rates. In 1961 these two programmes were superseded by a national Regional Development Fund, which now offers development loans and grants to areas that contain 43 per cent and 38 per cent of the national population respectively, occupying 93 per cent and 90 per cent of Norway. Only those areas around the Oslofjord and the next four largest towns of Bergen, Trondheim, Stavanger and Kristiansand were initially excluded. Regional incentives and agricultural subsidies were increased. The government's aims were to secure full employment, to protect the historic settlement pattern and to equalize living standards. This ambitious and expensive regional policy was relatively successful in the 1960s, with high rates of economic growth and a slow-growing labour force.

Since 1971, regional-development investment grants have been geographically differentiated according to need. Grants of up to 35 per cent could be offered in the Maximum Aid Areas in north Norway and some adjoining sections of the Trøndelag coast, compared with 25 per cent in the Special Development Areas in two coastal and most inland mountain parts of south Norway. Development areas offered 15 per cent grants in most of Sogn and Fjordane county and the Kongsvinger area on the Swedish border. The five main urban areas that are not eligible for assistance have development control in the form of industrial-development permits. In the northern half of north Norway, the limit for regional development grants has since been lifted to 40 per cent for Finnmark and the north-eastern part of Troms (Figure 5.2). Only loans and operating subsidies are available in the new Intermediate Areas in southern Norway. Some successful regional centres, such as Molde and Tromsø, have now lost all development assistance and are included in the Non-Designated Areas (Distriktenes Utbyggingsfond, 1990). Grants and loans totalled $50m in 1984. Regional plans are drawn up with the close co-operation of government and elected county councils and municipalities. Decisions are taken at county level on about half the regional development grants and loans by value. The Regional Development Fund can also support special occupational training, new-company non-investment project and start-up costs, marketing development and new-product development costs in small companies.

The government have given regional transport subsidies since 1971 of up to 40 per cent of the transport cost of sending finished and semi-finished manufactured goods from north Norway and the mid-west coast to markets more than 400 km away. These transport subsidies cost $15 million in 1984. The government also supports infrastructure development and gives tax concessions to individuals on industrial investment in regional development areas. Employer's payroll tax or social-security contributions are regionally reduced in all designated regional development areas at a cost, in 1984, of $140 million. Agriculture, fisheries, transport, State-owned companies, shipbuilding and some manufacturing are also subsidized, and tax equalization grants are given to local authorities. Norway's total annnual subsidy bill is the highest in Western Europe, at over $1,000 per capita in 1986−7; next comes Finland at $840 and then Sweden at $650 per capita. Reducing this high subsidy bill is a high priority for the new centre and right minority government elected in 1989 on a platform of reduced public expenditure and some privatization.

Regional policy retains its support across the political spectrum as urban roots are shallow in Norway. Norway only achieved an urban majority after the Second World War and most urban dwellers retain close rural links through family members or second homes. The 1972 referendum vote against EC membership was a rejection of urban Europe by a country with deep rural roots. The 'no' vote was strongest in the most rural and peripheral areas whose economy and way of life were threatened by the EC's common agriculture and fisheries policies.

The 1970s marked a watershed in Norway's regional population development. For the first time the Oslofjord counties experienced net out-migration, mainly to the benefit of the neighbouring south-west and eastern interior regions. The south-west now gained migrants from the south-east, as well as from all other regions, because of oil-industry activity centred on Stavanger and the south west's sunbelt location facing the European market. Norway's birth rate continued to fall in the 1970s and the volume of internal migration shrank as the supply of surplus rural labour from peripheral Norway dried up and regional development policy created local job opportunities. Some regional policy powers were decentralized to elected county councils. Municipal reform had reduced the number of municipalities from about 1,200 to 450 by 1970. This enabled the government to create a four-tier hierarchy of urban centres: the national capital, Oslo; major regional centres, such as Bergen, Trondheim and Tromsø, with a mixture of commercial and industrial employment and regional services, such as specialist hospitals and educational facilities; regional growth centres, which are the other county towns; and local centres, which are municipality centres. Regional growth centres were usually provided with regional airports, hospitals, secondary- and higher-education facilities, and are attractive locations for commerce and medium-sized industries. Local centres provide social services, primary education and local commercial and transport facilities. However, as Norway's counties have on average 50 per cent less population than Sweden's, and its municipalities only one third of the population of Sweden's, it has been harder to create viable third- and fourth-tier centres. In response to metropolitan domination, the government set up Norway's fourth university in the far north at Tromsø in 1972 and eleven regional higher-education colleges between 1969 and 1980. It also created the Oil Ministry at Stavanger and decentralized some civil service jobs to four other towns in southern Norway.

The quadrupling of well-head oil prices by OPEC in 1973 depressed the market for Norway's huge tanker fleet but boosted the profitability of Norway's infant oil industry. Many of Norway's 104 one-industry towns were already unprofitable by the 1970s, losing population as the younger generation had few local job prospects (Hansen, 1983). Norway's oil wealth created an artificially strong currency in the late 1970s, which helped to make Norway's forest products, metal smelting and chemical industries uncompetitive in world markets. From 1976 oil and gas revenues were used by government to subsidize industry. Although Norway's oil industry only accounts for 2 per cent of national employment, by 1983 it produced 15 per cent of GNP and one third of government tax revenue. This allowed a 40-per-cent expansion in service-sector employment in the 1970s, many part time in social services and health but spread throughout Norway.

The 1980s witnessed a partial return to the previous pattern of out-migration from north and west Norway to the Oslofjord area, but this time especially from declining one-industry towns and, in particular, fishing towns. This was highlighted in 1989 when the people of Bugøynes, a bankrupt Finnmark fishing village with 50 per cent unemployment, advertised in national newspapers to move *en bloc* elsewhere. Deindustrialization has paradoxically affected the larger, better-located urban areas most, for government subsidies have protected one-industry towns and remoter locations. Annual subsidies per worker averaged £7,000 in agriculture and £5,000 in fisheries. Unemployment rose to 3 per cent by 1983 and 4.9 per cent by 1990, low by European levels but a record high by post-war Norwegian standards. The government approved a crisis aid package for northern Norway as unemployment rose – for example, in Finnmark to a record 7.7 per cent in 1990, which was due to the near collapse of cod fisheries from overfishing by foreign factory trawlers in the Barents Sea.

Oil and gas wealth has allowed Norway to delay the rationalization of its outdated settlement pattern. However, rationalization is likely to resume in the 1990s when declining oil revenues and possible EC membership are likely to undermine many fishing and farming communities and one-industry towns.

5.5.4 Sweden

Counterurbanization began in the 1970s as Sweden's metropolitan areas lost 10,000 persons per year by net out migration, which marked a dramatic reversal of previous rural-to-urban and regional migration flows. It also provided evidence of the shift from an industrial society with its agglomeration tendencies to a post-industrial service-sector-dominated society. Manufacturing employment fell from 36 per cent in 1960 to 30 per cent in 1970 and 26 per cent in 1980 (see Table 1.4, p. 20).

Sweden had been the first Scandinavian country to develop an industrial economy. Its industrial activity initially focused on sawn timber products and on iron making using charcoal as the reducing agent. Widespread industrialization based on Sweden's varied but scattered resource base had, however, been delayed by the absence of significant coal deposits until the early twentieth century, when hydro-electricity was extensively developed. The parallel commercialization and mechanization of farming and forestry was responsible for decades of large-scale migration from rural areas, mainly to the three metropolitan areas of Stockholm, Gothenburg and Malmö. Employment in forestry, for example, fell from 250,000 in 1960 to 25,000 by the 1980s, although production increased as a result of mechanized tree felling and improved road transport. There was a much smaller corresponding loss in farming employment because of large government subsidies to agriculture. As a result, in the 1960s there was net outmigration of between 10,000 and 24,000 people per year from the eight northernmost and least-developed forestry-dominated counties to the metropolitan areas.

Sweden's formal regional development programme began in 1952 with the whole of northern Sweden designated as a development area by the social-democratic government, although assistance was concentrated on employment centres. Regional intervention had previously taken the form of specific government investments, such as railway building in the nineteenth century and the Inlandsban (Northern Interior Railway) in the 1930s to open up new land. The regional development programme became two tier in 1970 with greater assistance available in the least-developed northern interior. In response to metropolitan domination, new universities were opened at Umeå in 1963 and Linköping in 1970. Municipal reform had reduced the number of municipalities from about 2,500 to under 300. This enabled central government to create a four-tier hierarchy of urban centres in 1969: metropolitan areas, primary centres, regional centres and municipal centres. This structure was used for decentralizing employment from the three overdeveloped metropolitan areas of Stockholm, Gothenburg and Malmö, which had been draining talented people from the rest of Sweden. The main beneficiaries were the

23 county towns, called second-tier primary centres, which previously had inadequate opportunities for highly qualified and female labour. The most dramatic shift was the planned decentralization in the 1970s of 10,000 civil-service jobs, a quarter of the total, from Stockholm to 13 of the county towns (Oscarsson and Öberg, 1987). Deconcentration of power to administrative county boards with State-appointed governors also boosted the county towns. These county boards were also given some regional development power and funds amounting to 298 million SKr for regional development aid each year, mainly in northernmost Sweden. The decentralized expansion of health care and social services, further education and other public investment occurred mainly in the primary centres and in the regional centres, which provide employment and service facilities for more than one municipality. A very high 35 per cent of all Swedish employment is now in public-sector jobs, compared with 27 per cent in Norway and 24 per cent in Western Europe as a whole, but their distribution is remarkably equal among the counties, due to the planned decentralization of power and jobs to counties and municipalities.

The addition of a third, intermediate zone of regional development aid in 1973 reflected the decline of old-established industrial areas and the need for economic reconstruction in Bergslagen and other areas adjoining northern Sweden. The government also introduced regional transport subsidies of 10–50 per cent for northern Sweden, costing 242 million SKr per year by 1988, and passenger subsidies to firms requiring frequent personal contact with central and southern Sweden. There is also a subsidy to SJ to retain sleeper services to northern Sweden. From 1976, the deepening international recession undermined high-wage firms in some traditional industries, many located in one-industry towns. The 1976 centre and right Swedish government responded with emergency rescue packages to what it thought were temporary economic conditions, as traditional regional-development incentives act too slowly. Sweden delayed restructuring its industrial base for domestic political reasons by subsidizing and modernizing firms to improve productivity in threatened industries, such as shipbuilding, iron-ore mining, steel, textiles and parts of pulp and paper making. Shipbuilding alone absorbed tens of millions of Swedish krona of subsidy in a vain attempt at survival when the metropolitan labour markets of Malmö and Gothenburg were large enough to absorb many of the redundant shipbuilding workers.

In the 1980s Sweden, like Norway, reverted to its pre-1970 migration pattern of metropolitan gain and peripheral loss, but at much lower levels than before. Integrated regional planning was virtually abandoned after 1982 as market forces were given a greater role in reshaping the economy by the new social-democratic government. Regional development areas were also radically reduced in 1982 and now cover only 13.4 per cent of the national population (but 62 per cent of Sweden's area). Although the three-tiered system of special, ordinary and intermediate development areas was retained, with investment grants reducing from 50 per cent to 20 per cent respectively, most of coastal northern Sweden now became an intermediate area or lost its development status completely (Figure 5.2; Swedish Institute, 1988b). This was a reflection of the relative economic success of the expanded coastal towns and a vindication of thirty years of development aid concentrated upon growth centres.

The government has also created temporary development areas in districts outside the scheduled assisted areas that suffer short-term structural change. Here the government can direct extra resources to support private entrepreneurs and to improve local infrastructure and education. This scheme enabled Volvo to replace the shipyard at Uddevalla by a car-assembly plant.

Firms in the special development, development and intermediate areas who create new jobs receive employment grants of up to 40,000 SKr per employee (reducing to 10,000 after seven years). Most regional aid (Table 5.2) is channelled through the County Administrative Boards, which are also the main planning authorities, and the National Industries Board, which is in charge of the regional economic-forecasting system. Thinly populated areas with under 10 persons per km^2 are a continuing problem. Three-hundred thousand people live within small local labour markets with fewer than 30,000 people within 40 km of their main employment centre.

By the late 1980s employment in manufacturing industry was still falling and employment in many parts of the public sector had ceased to expand. The technical renewal of firms located in peripheral regions is

Table 5.2 Swedish regional development aid, 1988–9 (million Skr)

	Government and Industry Board	County Administrative Boards
Grants	362	353
Loans	200	—
Transport support	256	—
Sectoral support	—	150
Development projects	10	150
Technology centres	13	—

Source: Swedish Institute (1988b).

taking place more slowly than those in the cities. Substantial funds have therefore been allocated to higher education in Umeå, Luleå and Kiruna and also to twenty smaller technology centres scattered across the assisted areas. Just as the job gains of the 'cornerstone' industries of the 1960s (such as the Luleå steelworks) were confined to the towns in which they were founded, so the development effects of 'K' centres for information technology and data-processing – most notably Umeå in the public sector and Ludvika (Asea Brown Boveri) in the private sector – are very narrowly focused.

Regional development aid is only one among five categories of regional support. The largest expenditure is on job-training and pre-retirement schemes, scaled to the local level of unemployment, which together reduce unemployment by half. The second largest expenditure is on sectoral support to agriculture, manufacturing and services (including local shops) in sparsely populated areas, followed next by tax equalization grants to municipalities in order to increase the per-capita income tax yield to at least the national average and up to 35 per cent above it. Special crisis measures to stave off factory closures are the fourth category. An additional regional aid to the northernmost county of Norrbotten is the reduction and, in one area, the abolition, of payroll tax and social-security contributions for firms.

SIX

Conclusion

The Scandinavian countries are now among the most prosperous in Europe and in the forefront of the change to a post-industrial society based on information technology and a wide range of services. Nevertheless, they face a number of choices and problems in adjusting to the likely economic and social conditions of the early twenty-first century. Some of these problems, such as the growing proportion of the elderly population and the need to expand services in order to provide for them, are shared with all developed economies. Others are characteristic of small countries, especially the extent to which the maintenance of high living standards depends on selling goods and services abroad. Yet others can be related to the long historical semi-isolation of much of Scandinavia from the main currents of European social and economic life. This has led not only to a widespread belief in the possibility of social harmony and consensus but also to a residue of suspicion towards the Europe of Germany, France and Italy.

The 1990s may offer another opportunity to choose between full membership of the EC and a looser relationship similar to that between Canada and the USA. The EC market of almost 360 million people offers the best and nearest opportunities for trade but it is unrealistic to expect that the EC would modify its hard-won internal compromises in order to take account of the interest of 17 million Scandinavians. For Norway and Sweden to enter, therefore, would involve drastic changes in agricultural and fisheries policies. If Norwegian and Swedish manufacturing industries were to compete within the Common Market they would be hampered by their relatively high inflation and interest rates, rising wages, slow growth in productivity and uncertainty concerning future supplies of energy. Entry to the EC might also involve compromises in economic organization and social structure. A vocal minority of Scandinavians argue that their countries are already wealthy enough and should pioneer a distinctly Scandinavian 'post-industrial' life-style in which the 'Nordic Model' of social democracy would be developed further, with more emphasis upon equality of opportunity, the improvement of the environment, the redistribution of wealth through high personal taxation and a large public-service sector.

The 1990s will bring other economic challenges. Increasing international competition makes it essential to maintain the educational and social infrastructure that enables goods and services of the highest quality to be offered to the world market and to retain the profits from such activity within Scandinavia. The labour markets and tax systems may need to be modified so that internationally competitive industrial sectors are not starved of labour and investment. Public services must be brought to a high level of efficiency without allowing market forces to have too big a say in welfare provision.

Scandinavian think-tanks have found it difficult to quantify the trade-off between the preservation of current Scandinavian values and patterns of settlement and the maintenance of the efficiency needed to compete in foreign markets. Market forces drive powerfully in a centralizing direction. This is already evident in the transformation of former government agencies to commercial concerns. Major State investments in infrastructure (such as the re-organization of public transport in east central Sweden and in the Oslo area) encourage large, new, private investments in the same areas, drawn thither by the new market values created. A scenario relying more strongly upon market forces threatens a growing wealth and opportunity gap between the urbanized regions within 100 km of the five major cities (along with regional capitals, such as Århus, Bergen, Trondheim and Jönköping) and the rest of Scandinavia. Emigration from the northern periphery of Scandinavia and its remoter islands, such as Gotland and Bornholm, would be strongly encouraged.

In many peripheral areas of Norway and Sweden north of 60°, but also in parts of Småland, south-east Sweden, north and west Jutland and the smaller Danish islands, the population is already at the minimum required to support modern health and educational services within a reasonable journey. If the number of graduates continues to grow to levels found in North America at the present day, it will be essential to provide satisfying graduate employment in the peripheral regions on a wider scale than that already available at such centres as Trondheim, Umeå and Tromsø. The full integration of the periphery into the economic life of post-industrial Scandinavia would require more State investment and direction, not only in education, health and transport but also in housing and economic support systems. How is the wealth to be generated to pay for so much investment, and how is it to be transferred from the core to the periphery?

An EC administering the large regional development funds envisaged by social-democratic supporters of the EC would expect substantial contributions from the affluent northern nations. How far are Scandinavians prepared to help raise Aegean or eastern-German living standards while trying to ensure equality of opportunity between central and peripheral Scandinavia? The 1990s seem likely to test the Scandinavian ideals of rational argument, consensual organization and social cohesion to their limits.

REFERENCES

Annual Abstract of Statistics (1988) HMSO, London.

Bachtler, J. and Bienkowski, M. (1988) Regional policy reviews in Denmark: Assisted Area redesignation and the new Regional Development Act, *Regional Science Association Newsletter*, no. 156, pp. 4–7.

Bielckus, C. L. (1977) Second homes in Scandinavia, in J. T. Coppock (ed.) *Second Homes, Curse or Blessing?*, Pergamon Press, Oxford.

Bjørkvik, H. (1963) Norwegian seter-farming, *Scandinavian Economic History Review*, Vol. XI, no. 2, pp. 156–66.

Brækhus, K. (1976) Oslo: past, present and future, *Norsk Geografisk Tidsskrift*, Vol. 30, pp. 127–38.

City of Copenhagen (1973) *København: A Short Description of the Origin of Copenhagen, the City's Physical Structure and Planning*, City Engineer's Department, City Architect's Department and Copenhagen General Planning Department, Copenhagen.

Clout, H. D. (ed.) (1975) *Regional Development in Western Europe*, Wiley, Chichester.

Connery, D. S. (1966) *The Scandinavians*, Eyre & Spottiswoode, London.

Coull, J. R. (1971) *Crofter-Fishermen in Norway and Scotland* (O'Dell Memorial Monograph no. 2), Department of Geography, University of Aberdeen.

Court, Y. (1987) Denmark, in H. D. Clout (ed.) *Regional Development in Western Europe* (3rd edn), Fulton, London.

Court, Y. (1989) Denmark: towards a more deconcentrated settlement pattern, in A. G. Champion (ed.) *Counterurbanization: The Changing Pace and Nature of Population Deconcentration*, Edward Arnold, London, Chap. 7.

Daun, A. (1985) Setbacks and advances in the Swedish housing market, *Current Sweden*, no. 331, Swedish Institute, Stockholm.

Denmark Review (1988) no. 3/88, Royal Danish Ministry of Foreign Affairs, Copenhagen.

Denmark Review (1989) no. 1/89, Royal Danish Ministry of Foreign Affairs, Copenhagen.

Derry, T. K. (1979) *A History of Scandinavia*, Allen & Unwin, London.

Diem, A. (1965) An alternative to unplanned urban growth: the case of Stockholm, *Canadian Geographer*, Vol. IX, no. 4, pp. 193–204.

Diem, A. (1973) The growth and planning of Copenhagen, *Revue de Géographie de Montréal*, Vol. 27, pp. 41–51.

Distriktenes Utbyggingsfond (1990) Distriktenes Utbyggingsfond-Geografisk virkeområde, Distriktenes Utbyggingsfond, Oslo (September).

The Economist (1990) Swedish business, 17 November, p. 123.

Edin, K.-A. (1987) Sweden after Chernobyl: consequences of the nuclear accident, *Current Sweden*, no. 353, Swedish Institute, Stockholm.

Eduards, M. L. (1989) Women's participation and equal opportunities policies, *Current Sweden*, no. 369, Swedish Institute, Stockholm.

EFTA (1979) Norway's North Sea oil and gas: rapid expansion continues, *EFTA Bulletin*, Vol. XX, no. 7, pp. 12–14, Geneva.

Falk, T. (1976) *Urban Sweden*, Economic Research Institute, Stockholm School of Economics, Stockholm.

Fullerton, B. (1990) Deregulation in a European context – the case of Sweden, in P. Bell and P. Cloke (eds.) *Deregulation in Transport*, Fulton, London.

Glyn Jones, W. (1986) *Denmark, A Modern History*, Croom Helm, London.

Gustafsson, A. (1988) *Local Government in Sweden*, Swedish Institute, Stockholm.

Haavio-Mannila, E. *et al.* (eds.) (1985) *Unfinished Democracy – Women in Nordic Politics*, Pergamon Press, Oxford.

Hansen, J. C. (1983) Regional policy in an oil economy: the case of Norway, *Geoforum*, Vol. 14, no. 4, pp. 353–61.

Hansen, J. C. (1989) Norway: the turnaround which turned round, in A. G. Champion (ed.) *Counterurbanization: The Changing Pace and Nature of Population Deconcentration*, Edward Arnold, London, Chap. 6.

Hansen, P., Rying, B. and Borre, T. (1985) *Women in Denmark in the 1980s*, Royal Danish Ministry of Foreign Affairs, Copenhagen.

Hansen, V. (1960) Some characteristics of a growing suburban region, *Geografisk Tidsskrift*, Vol. 59, pp. 214–25.

Helle, E. (1989) Norway as an oil producer, *Norinform*, no. 233, Royal Norwegian Ministry of Foreign Affairs, Oslo.

Hernes, H. M. (1988) The Welfare State citizenship of Scandinavian women, in K. B. Jones and A. G. Jónasdóttir (eds.) *The Political Interests of Gender*, Sage, London, Chap. 9.

Hernes, H. M. and Hänninen-Salmelin, E. (1985) Women in the corporate System, in E. Haavio-Mannila *et al.* (eds.) *Unfinished Democracy – Women in Nordic Politics*, Pergamon Press, Oxford.

Hodne, F. (1975) *An Economic History of Norway 1815–1970*, Tapir, Bergen.

Hodne, F. (1983) *The Norwegian Economy 1920–80*, Croom Helm, Beckenham.

Illeris, S. (1990) Counter-urbanization revisited; the new map of population distribution in central and north-western Europe, *Norsk Geografisk Tidsskrift*, Vol. 44, pp. 39–52.

Jensen, K. (1984) *The Green Wedges of the Capital*, Greater Copenhagen Council and Ministry of the Environment Planning Department, Copenhagen.

Johansen, H. C. (1986) *The Danish Economy in the Twentieth Century*, Routledge, London.

John, B. (1984) *Scandinavia – A New Geography*, Longman, London.

Jörberg, L. (1973) The Nordic countries, 1850–1914, in C. M. Cipolla (ed.) *The Fontana Economic History of Europe*, Collins, Glasgow, Vol. 4.2.

Jörberg, L. and Krantz, O. (1975) Scandinavia, 1914–1970, in C. M. Cipolla (ed.) *The Fontana Economic History of Europe*, Collins, Glasgow, Vol. 6.2.

Kampp, Aa. H. (1987) Population and settlement in Denmark, in U. Varjo and W. Tietze (eds.) *Norden: Man and Environment*, Gebrüder Borntraeger, Stuttgart, pp. 213–24.

Kesselman, M. and Krieger, J. (eds.) (1987) *European Politics in Transition*, Heath, Lexington, Mass.

Knowles, R. D. (1981) Malapportionment in Norway's parliamentary elections since 1921, *Norsk Geografisk Tidsskrift*, Vol. 35, pp. 147–59.

Knowles, R. D. (1985) Scandinavia's energy boom, *Geo*, Vol. 8, no. 2, pp. 4, 5, 8.

Københavns Statistiske Årbog (1987) Copenhagen Statistical Office, Copenhagen.

Lemberg, K. (1973) *Pedestrian Streets and other Motor Vehicle Traffic Restraints in Central Copenhagen*, General Planning Department, City of Copenhagen.

Lewan, N. (1987) Populations and settlement in Sweden, in U. Varjo and W. Tietze (eds.) *Norden: Man and Environment*, Gebrüder Borntraeger, Stuttgart, pp. 256–66.

Matthiessen, C. W. (1980) Trends in the urbanization process; the Copenhagen case, *Geografisk Tidsskrift*, Vol. 80, pp. 98–101.

Mead, W. R. (1958) *An Economic Geography of the Scandinavian States and Finland*, University of London Press.

Mead, W. R. (1981) *An Historical Geography of Scandinavia*, Academic Press, London.

Ministry of Church and Education (1989) *Education in Norway*, Ministry of Church and Education and Ministry of Cultural and Scientific Affairs, Oslo.

Ministry of Education (1990) *Education in Denmark*, Copenhagen.

Ministry of Housing (1974) *Housing in Denmark*, Copenhagen.

Ministry of Local Government and Labour (1982) *Housing in Norway*, Oslo.

Muniz, I., Seip, H. M. and Samstag, T. (1989) *Acid Rain: Time for Action*, Ministry of the Environment, Oslo.

Myklebost, H. (1960) Norges tettbygde steder 1875–1950, *Ad Novas 4*, Universitetsforlaget, Oslo-Bergen.

Myklebost, H. (1976) The decrease of fertility in Norway: the spread of an innovation, *Norsk Geografisk Tidsskrift*, Vol. 30, pp. 179–86.

Myklebost, H. (1984) The evidence for urban turnaround in Norway, *Geoforum*, Vol. 5, no. 2, pp. 161–76.

Nesheim, A. (1981) The Lapps of Norway and their history, *Norway Information*, no. 309, Royal Norwegian Ministry of Foreign Affairs, Oslo.

Nordic Council of Ministers (1989) *Stronger Nordic Countries Economic Action Plan 1989–92*, Copenhagen.

Norling, G. E. (1960) Abandonment of rural settlement in Västerbotten Lappmark, North Sweden 1930–1960, *Geografiska Annaler*, Vol. XLII, pp. 232–43.

OECD Economic Surveys: Sweden (1988–9); Denmark (1989–90); Norway (1989–90) OECD, Paris.

Oscarsson, G. and Öberg, S. (1987) Northern Europe, in H. D. Clout (ed.) *Regional Development in Western Europe* (3rd edn), Fulton, London.

Pollard, S. (1981) *Peaceful Conquest – The Industrialization of Europe 1760–1970*, Oxford University Press.

Pooley, C. G. (1989) Working class housing in European cities since 1850, in R. Lawton (ed.) *The Rise and Fall of Great Cities: Aspects of Urbanization in the Western World*, Belhaven, London, Chap. 8.

Rasmussen, T. F. (1965) The development of a planned plurinuclear city region: Greater Oslo (Regional Science Association, Papers, XVI), Cracow Congress.

Rasmussen, T. F. (1985) 'Contemporary Norway: its economy and politics' and 'Norway's urban future' in J. S. Torstenson, M. F. Metcalf and T. F. Rasmussen, *Urbanization and Community Building in Modern Norway*, Urbana Press, Oslo.

Royal Danish Ministry of Health (1987) *Health Care in Denmark (Facts about Denmark)*, Royal Danish Ministry of Foreign Affairs, Copenhagen.

Royal Ministry of Petroleum and Energy (1990) *The Norwegian Continental Shelf 1990* (fact-sheet), Oslo.

Rydén, B. and Bergstrom, V. (eds.) (1982) *Sweden: Choices for Economic and Social Policy in the 1980s*, Allen & Unwin, London.

Schierbeck, O. (1990) The high price of life in Utopia, *Guardian*, 30 November (reprinted from *Politiken*, Denmark).

Showstack-Sassoon, A. (ed.) (1987) *Women and the State: Contradictions of the Welfare State*, Hutchinson, London.

Sidenbladh, G. (1965) Stockholm: a planned city, in G. Sidenbladh (ed.) *Cities, a Scientific American Book*, Penguin Books, Harmondsworth.

Sinkkonen, S. (1985) Local politics, in E. Haavio-Mannila *et al.* (eds.) *Unfinished Democracy – Women in Nordic Politics*, Pergamon Press, Oxford.

Smith, A. D. (1991) A new law to protect a language, *Guardian*, 1 February.

Sømme, A. (ed.) (1960) *The Geography of Norden*, Cappelen, Oslo.

Stange, D. (1990) The Norwegian education system, *Norinform*, no. 347, Royal Norwegian Ministry of Foreign Affairs, Oslo.

Statistisk Årbog Danmark (1989) Danmarks Statistik, Copenhagen.

Statistisk Årbok Norway (1988 and 1989) Central Bureau of Statistics of Norway, Oslo and Kongsvinger.

Statistisk Årsbok Sweden (1988 and 1990) Statistiska Centralbyrån, Stockholm.

Stenstadvold, K. (1977) Regional and structural effects of North Sea oil in Norway, *Geojournal*, Vol. 1, no. 1, pp. 71–93.

Stone, K. H. (1962) Swedish fringes of settlement, *Annals of the Association of American Geographers*, Vol. 52, pp. 373–93.

Stone, K. H. (1965) The development of a focus for the geography of settlement, *Economic Geography*, Vol. 41, pp. 346–55.

Stone, K. H. (1971) *Norway's Internal Migration to New Farms Since 1920*, Martinns Nijhoff, The Hague.

Strand, T. (1976) *Geographic Policies – a Comparative Study of Norway and Sweden*, Institute of Social Studies, Bergen University.

Strath, B. (1987) *The Politics of Deindustrialisation – the Contraction of the West European Shipbuilding Industry*, Routledge, London.

Sund, T. (1960) Norway, in A. Sømme (ed.) *The Geography of Norden*, Heinemann, London, Chap. 11.

Swedish Institute (1987) *Primary and Secondary Education in Sweden (Fact-Sheets on Sweden)*, Stockholm.

Swedish Institute (1988a) *Agriculture in Sweden* (*Fact-Sheets on Sweden*), Stockholm.

Swedish Institute (1988b) *Swedish Regional Policy* (*Fact-Sheets on Sweden*), Stockholm.

Swedish Institute (1988c) *Forestry and Forest Industry* (*Fact-Sheets on Sweden*), Stockholm.

Swedish Institute (1988d) *Environment Protection* (*Fact-Sheets on Sweden*), Stockholm.

Swedish Institute (1988e) *The Lapps in Sweden* (*Fact-Sheets on Sweden*), Stockholm.

Swedish Institute (1989a) *Higher Education in Sweden* (*Fact-Sheets on Sweden*), Stockholm.

Swedish Institute (1989b) *Health and Medical Care in Sweden* (*Fact-Sheets on Sweden*), Stockholm.

Swedish Institute (1989c) *Immigrants in Sweden* (*Fact-Sheets on Sweden*), Stockholm.

Taylor, J. G. (1974) Scandinavian cooperation in the production and distribution of electricity, *Norsk Geografisk Tidsskrift*, Vol. 28, pp. 61–76.

Toft-Jensen, H. (1982) The role of the State in regional development, planning and implementation: the case of Denmark, in R. Hudson and J. R. Lewis (eds.) *Regional Planning in Europe*, Pion, London, pp. 127–47.

Törnqvist, G. (ed.) (1986) *Svenskt näringsliv i geografiskt perspektiv*, Liber, Stockholm.

Torstenson, J. S., Metcalf, M. F. and Rasmussen, T. F. (1985) *Urbanization and Community Building in Modern Norway*, Urbana Press, Oslo.

Transportarbeidet i Norden (1980) Nordisk Komité for Transportøkonomisk Forskning, Copenhagen.

Varjo, U. and Tietze, W. (eds.) (1987) *Norden: Man and Environment*, Borntræger, Berlin.

von Würtemberg, J. M. (1987) The cost of present agricultural policies in the EFTA countries (occasional paper no. 18), EFTA, Geneva.

Yearbook of Nordic Statistics (1981, 1988 and 1989–90) Nordic Statistical Secretariat, Copenhagen.

PLACE INDEX

SUBJECT INDEX